CRACK THE AI INTERVIEW

Deep Learning, AI, and Machine Learning Questions with Case Studies.

Answer Tough Questions, Solve Complex Problems, and Stand Out

By

Samuel Hall

Contents

Introduction

Artificial intelligence (AI) is no longer just a buzzword; it's reshaping industries, creating opportunities, and presenting unique challenges. For professionals pursuing a career in AI, acing interviews in this domain has become both a critical step and a daunting task. Unlike traditional tech interviews, AI-focused interviews require a blend of theoretical understanding, practical problem-solving, and a deep grasp of real-world applications. This book is your guide to navigating that intricate landscape.

Why AI Interviews Are Unique

AI interviews differ from standard software engineering or data science interviews in several ways. The role of an AI professional often blends data engineering, machine learning, and systems design with a strong focus on innovation. As a result, the interview process tests a combination of theoretical expertise, coding proficiency, and creative problem-solving.

Some aspects that make AI interviews distinct include:

- **A Multi-Disciplinary Approach:** Expect questions that span mathematics (linear algebra, probability), computer science fundamentals (algorithms, data structures), and domain-specific knowledge (NLP, computer vision).
- **Hands-On Challenges:** Many interviews feature coding exercises that focus on building, debugging, or optimizing machine learning models.
- **System Design with AI Integration:** Beyond designing systems, you'll need to demonstrate how AI components fit into larger architectures, such as a chatbot pipeline or recommendation system.

- **Emphasis on Practicality:** Employers often assess your ability to apply AI knowledge to real-world scenarios, from handling messy data to designing scalable AI systems.
- **Ethical Considerations:** Increasingly, companies expect candidates to consider fairness, bias, and transparency when proposing AI solutions.

These unique demands mean that AI interviews not only test your technical expertise but also your ability to adapt, innovate, and think holistically about AI's role in solving business problems.

Key Challenges in AI Interviews

1. **Breadth of Knowledge Required:**
   AI is a vast field, and interviewers often cover a wide range of topics, from regression models to generative adversarial networks. Balancing depth and breadth in your preparation can feel overwhelming.

2. **Unpredictable Problem-Solving Scenarios:**
   Unlike traditional coding challenges, AI interviews often present open-ended questions like, "How would you design a fraud detection system for an e-commerce platform?" These scenarios require creative thinking and an ability to break down complex problems.

3. **Data-Centric Thinking:**
   Many questions focus on working with real-world datasets, which are often noisy and incomplete. Candidates must demonstrate data preprocessing, feature engineering, and model selection skills.

4. **Interpreting Results:**
   Understanding metrics like precision, recall, and F1 score is just the beginning. Interviewers want to see

your ability to evaluate model performance, debug issues, and iterate effectively.

5. **Time Pressure:**
   Solving complex problems while articulating your thought process under time constraints is a challenge in itself.

How This Book Helps

This book is designed to address these challenges and equip you with the tools, techniques, and confidence to excel in AI interviews. Here's how:

- **Comprehensive Coverage:** Each chapter delves into critical AI topics, breaking down complex concepts into digestible explanations with practical examples.
- **Real-World Case Studies:** To bridge theory and practice, we've included case studies that mimic actual interview scenarios. These will help you understand how to tackle challenges like designing a recommendation engine or building an image classification system.
- **Code Examples with Explanations:** Functional, well-commented code snippets illustrate key algorithms and techniques. You'll learn not just *what* works but *why* it works and *how* to apply it.
- **Behavioral Skills:** Technical skills are only part of the equation. This book also offers guidance on answering behavioral questions, negotiating offers, and showcasing teamwork and leadership in your AI projects.
- **Mock Interviews and Practice Questions:** Practice makes perfect. The book includes mock

interviews and practice problems tailored to AI roles, giving you the confidence to tackle tough questions.

- **Actionable Insights:** Based on best practices and lessons learned from successful AI professionals, the book offers practical advice to help you stand out in competitive interviews.

AI interviews may be tough, but with the right preparation, they're conquerable. This book isn't just about passing an interview; it's about understanding the field, showcasing your expertise, and positioning yourself as a standout candidate. Whether you're aiming to become a machine learning engineer, a data scientist, or an AI researcher, this guide will serve as your roadmap to success.

Let's get started. Your journey to mastering AI interviews begins now.

Chapter 1: Foundations of AI and ML

Artificial Intelligence (AI) and Machine Learning (ML) have become cornerstones of modern technology. Whether it's personal assistants like Siri, recommendation systems on Netflix, or autonomous vehicles, these fields shape the way we interact with technology. To ace AI interviews, a strong understanding of foundational concepts is essential. This chapter provides an overview of the core terminologies, tools, and techniques you'll need, along with a practical case study to solidify your knowledge.

1.1 Core Concepts and Terminologies

Artificial Intelligence (AI) and Machine Learning (ML) are vast fields, but understanding their foundational concepts is crucial to mastering them. In this section, we'll break down key terminologies, present their relationships, and provide actionable insights into why these concepts matter in real-world applications.

What is AI?

Artificial Intelligence refers to systems designed to perform tasks that typically require human intelligence, such as problem-solving, decision-making, and language understanding. The goal of AI is not just to mimic human behavior but to perform these tasks at scale and with efficiency that exceeds human capabilities.

Key AI Domains:

- **Computer Vision**: Enabling machines to interpret visual data.
- **Natural Language Processing (NLP)**: Understanding and generating human language.
- **Robotics**: Automating physical tasks.
- **Expert Systems**: Emulating decision-making in specialized domains.

Machine Learning (ML) Overview

Machine Learning is a subset of AI that focuses on building systems that learn and improve from data without explicit programming.

Key ML Categories:

- **Supervised Learning**: Uses labeled data to predict outcomes. Example: Predicting house prices.
- **Unsupervised Learning**: Identifies patterns in unlabeled data. Example: Clustering customer behaviors.
- **Reinforcement Learning**: Trains agents to make decisions through rewards and penalties. Example: Training robots in dynamic environments.

Deep Learning

Deep Learning, a subset of ML, leverages neural networks with multiple layers to process and analyze complex patterns in large datasets. Applications include image recognition, NLP, and speech processing.

Key Terminologies in AI and ML

1. **Feature Engineering**: Selecting or creating meaningful inputs for a model.
2. **Model Training**: Teaching a model to identify patterns in data.
3. **Overfitting and Underfitting**:
   - **Overfitting**: The model is too tailored to training data and performs poorly on unseen data.
   - **Underfitting**: The model is too simplistic to capture underlying trends.
4. **Hyperparameters**: Settings that define model behavior, such as learning rate and batch size.
5. **Optimization Algorithms**: Techniques like Gradient Descent to minimize errors during training.

Practical Example: Decision Trees

A Decision Tree is a simple yet powerful supervised learning algorithm. It splits data into branches based on conditions to reach a prediction. For instance, consider an AI that predicts whether a customer will buy a product based on age and income.

How it works:

1. The tree starts with the root node (e.g., all customers).
2. At each decision point, data is split based on a feature threshold (e.g., age > 30).
3. This continues until reaching leaf nodes, representing outcomes (e.g., "Buy" or "Not Buy").

Key Metrics for Model Evaluation

- **Accuracy**: Percentage of correctly classified data points.
- **Precision and Recall**: Measures model performance on imbalanced datasets.
- **F1-Score**: A balanced measure combining precision and recall.
- **Confusion Matrix**: Visualizes true positives, true negatives, and errors.

Case Study: Credit Card Fraud Detection

Building an ML system to detect fraudulent transactions highlights the importance of understanding foundational concepts.

1. **Problem Statement**: Identify anomalies in financial transactions to flag potential fraud.
2. **Dataset**: Contains features like transaction amount, location, and time.
3. **Model**: Random Forest, a robust algorithm for classification tasks.
4. **Evaluation**: Use precision-recall curves to optimize for minimal false positives.

1.2 Tools and Libraries for ML and AI

The rapid development of AI and ML relies heavily on the availability of powerful tools and libraries. These resources simplify the implementation of complex algorithms, enhance productivity, and enable engineers and researchers to build scalable, cutting-edge systems. This chapter provides an overview of essential tools and libraries, their unique features, and practical guidance on their application.

Programming Languages for AI and ML

- **Python**: The most popular language due to its simplicity and an extensive ecosystem of libraries.
- **R**: Preferred for statistical computing and data visualization.
- **Julia**: Known for high-performance numerical computing.
- **Java and C++**: Often used in large-scale production systems.

Key Libraries and Frameworks

Below is a categorized list of must-know tools:

1. General Machine Learning

- **Scikit-learn**: A beginner-friendly library for classical ML algorithms.
- **XGBoost**: Known for gradient boosting in structured datasets.
- **H2O.ai**: Designed for scalable machine learning applications.

2. Deep Learning

- **TensorFlow**: A versatile framework by Google for neural networks and production-grade ML.
- **PyTorch**: A flexible, developer-friendly library popular for research and prototyping.
- **Keras**: Built on top of TensorFlow, focusing on simplicity and ease of use.

3. Natural Language Processing (NLP)

- **spaCy**: For industrial-strength NLP.
- **Hugging Face Transformers**: Provides pre-trained models for tasks like text classification and language translation.
- **NLTK**: Useful for basic NLP tasks such as tokenization and stemming.

4. Computer Vision

- **OpenCV**: For real-time image processing and computer vision tasks.
- **fastai**: Built on PyTorch, it simplifies vision and text model training.

5. Data Manipulation and Visualization

- **Pandas**: For efficient data manipulation and analysis.
- **Matplotlib and Seaborn**: For generating insightful visualizations.
- **Plotly**: For interactive, web-based visualizations.

Integrated Development Environments (IDEs)

- **Jupyter Notebook**: Interactive coding with inline visualizations.
- **Google Colab**: A cloud-based notebook supporting GPU/TPU acceleration.
- **VS Code**: Lightweight and extensible for any development environment.

Cloud Platforms for AI

- **Google AI Platform**: Offers TensorFlow processing power on the cloud.

- **AWS SageMaker**: A comprehensive suite for deploying machine learning models.
- **Azure Machine Learning**: Integrated tools for training and deploying at scale.

Case Study: Sentiment Analysis Using Hugging Face Transformers

Let's explore how tools like Hugging Face can simplify NLP workflows.

Problem: Build a sentiment analysis system to classify customer reviews as positive or negative.

Steps:

1. **Set up Environment**: Install Hugging Face and Transformers library.
2. **Load Pre-trained Model**: Use a BERT-based model fine-tuned for sentiment analysis.
3. **Preprocess Data**: Tokenize the text into input format.
4. **Run Predictions**: Use the model to classify sentiment.

Code Example:

python

```python
from transformers import pipeline

# Load pre-trained sentiment analysis model

classifier = pipeline("sentiment-analysis")
```

```python
# Input text
reviews = ["I love this product!", "This service is terrible."]

# Perform sentiment analysis
results = classifier(reviews)

# Display results
for review, result in zip(reviews, results):
    print(f"Review: {review} \nSentiment: {result['label']} (Score: {result['score']:.2f})\n")
```

Explanation:

- The `pipeline` simplifies the integration of pre-trained models.
- Input text is tokenized automatically.
- Outputs include the sentiment label and confidence score.

Case Study: Building a Simple Spam Classifier

Building a spam classifier is a classic and practical project in machine learning. This case study demonstrates how to design, train, and evaluate a simple spam classifier using Python. The process involves data preprocessing, feature extraction, model training, and evaluation.

Objective

Develop a binary classification model to identify whether an email message is spam or not.

Step 1: Dataset Preparation

Use a publicly available dataset such as the SMS Spam Collection. This dataset includes labeled text messages categorized as either "spam" or "ham" (not spam).

Code:

python

```python
import pandas as pd

# Load dataset
url = "https://raw.githubusercontent.com/datasets/sms-spam-collection/master/sms.csv"

data = pd.read_csv(url)

# Check data

print(data.head())
```

Step 2: Text Preprocessing

Preprocess the data by cleaning and tokenizing the text.

Tasks:

- Convert text to lowercase.
- Remove special characters and stopwords.
- Tokenize and vectorize the text using techniques like TF-IDF.

Code:

python

```python
from sklearn.feature_extraction.text import TfidfVectorizer

from sklearn.model_selection import train_test_split


# Extract labels and messages

X = data['message']

y = data['label']


# Split data

X_train, X_test, y_train, y_test = train_test_split(X, y, test_size=0.3, random_state=42)
```

```python
# Apply TF-IDF

vectorizer                                        =
TfidfVectorizer(stop_words='english',
max_features=3000)

X_train_vec                                       =
vectorizer.fit_transform(X_train)

X_test_vec = vectorizer.transform(X_test)
```

Step 3: Model Selection and Training

Train a simple model such as Naive Bayes, which performs well
with text classification tasks.

Code:

python

```python
from sklearn.naive_bayes import MultinomialNB

# Initialize and train the model

model = MultinomialNB()

model.fit(X_train_vec, y_train)


# Evaluate the model
```

```python
accuracy = model.score(X_test_vec, y_test)

print(f"Model    Accuracy:    {accuracy    *
100:.2f}%")
```

Step 4: Testing the Classifier

Test the classifier on unseen messages and analyze the results.

Code:

python

```python
# Test the model

sample_messages = ["Congratulations, you've
won a prize!", "Can we meet tomorrow?"]

sample_vec                                  =
vectorizer.transform(sample_messages)

predictions = model.predict(sample_vec)


for message, label in zip(sample_messages,
predictions):

    print(f"Message: {message} \nPrediction:
{label}\n")
```

Step 5: Model Evaluation

Measure performance using metrics like precision, recall, and F1-score.

Code:

python

```python
from          sklearn.metrics          import
classification_report


# Generate predictions

y_pred = model.predict(X_test_vec)


# Display evaluation metrics

print(classification_report(y_test, y_pred))
```

Chapter 2: Machine Learning in Action

2.1 Types of ML: Supervised, Unsupervised, and Reinforcement Learning

Machine learning (ML) is a diverse field encompassing various methodologies designed to address unique challenges. This section explores the three main paradigms of ML—Supervised, Unsupervised, and Reinforcement Learning—highlighting their fundamental concepts, real-world applications, and technical nuances.

Supervised Learning

Supervised learning is the most commonly used ML paradigm. It involves training a model on a labeled dataset, where each input has a corresponding output. The model learns a mapping function from inputs to outputs, enabling it to make predictions on new data.

Core Concepts

- **Input Features (X):** Independent variables used to make predictions.
- **Labels (Y):** Dependent variables or outcomes the model learns to predict.
- **Training Process:** Minimizing error (e.g., Mean Squared Error for regression or Cross-Entropy Loss for classification).

Applications

1. **Image Classification:** Identifying objects in images, such as distinguishing cats from dogs.
2. **Spam Detection:** Filtering emails based on their content.
3. **Medical Diagnosis:** Predicting diseases from patient data.

Popular Algorithms

- Linear Regression
- Logistic Regression
- Support Vector Machines (SVM)
- Decision Trees and Random Forests
- Neural Networks (e.g., Convolutional Neural Networks for image tasks)

Code Example: Spam Detection Using Logistic Regression

Here's a simple implementation of a spam classifier:

python

```python
import pandas as pd

from sklearn.model_selection import train_test_split

from sklearn.feature_extraction.text import CountVectorizer

from sklearn.linear_model import LogisticRegression

from sklearn.metrics import accuracy_score
```

```python
# Load dataset
data = pd.read_csv('spam.csv')
X = data['message']
y = data['label']


# Preprocess text data
vectorizer = CountVectorizer()
X_vectorized = vectorizer.fit_transform(X)


# Split dataset
X_train, X_test, y_train, y_test =
train_test_split(X_vectorized, y,
test_size=0.2, random_state=42)


# Train Logistic Regression model
model = LogisticRegression()
model.fit(X_train, y_train)


# Evaluate model
y_pred = model.predict(X_test)
```

```
print("Accuracy:",       accuracy_score(y_test,
y_pred))
```

Insights

- The CountVectorizer converts text into numerical representations (bag-of-words).
- Logistic Regression predicts whether a message is spam or not.

Unsupervised Learning

Unsupervised learning works on datasets without labeled outcomes. The goal is to uncover hidden patterns, groupings, or structures within the data.

Core Concepts

- **Clustering:** Grouping similar data points together.
- **Dimensionality Reduction:** Reducing data complexity while retaining significant information.

Applications

1. **Customer Segmentation:** Grouping customers based on purchasing behaviors.
2. **Anomaly Detection:** Identifying unusual patterns in data, such as fraud.
3. **Data Visualization:** Simplifying data for easy interpretation using PCA or t-SNE.

Popular Algorithms

- K-Means Clustering
- DBSCAN (Density-Based Spatial Clustering)
- Principal Component Analysis (PCA)

Code Example: Clustering Customers Using K-Means
Here's how K-Means clustering can segment customers:

python

```python
from sklearn.cluster import KMeans

import pandas as pd

import matplotlib.pyplot as plt


# Load customer data

data = pd.read_csv('customers.csv')

X = data[['annual_income', 'spending_score']]


# Train K-Means model

kmeans = KMeans(n_clusters=3, random_state=42)

data['cluster'] = kmeans.fit_predict(X)


# Visualize clusters

plt.scatter(data['annual_income'],
data['spending_score'],    c=data['cluster'],
cmap='viridis')

plt.xlabel('Annual Income')
```

```
plt.ylabel('Spending Score')

plt.title('Customer Segmentation')

plt.show()
```

Insights

- Customers are segmented into clusters based on income and spending habits.
- Visualizing the clusters provides actionable insights for targeted marketing.

Reinforcement Learning

Reinforcement learning (RL) is fundamentally different from supervised and unsupervised learning. It involves an agent interacting with an environment and learning to perform tasks by maximizing cumulative rewards.

Core Concepts

- **Agent:** The decision-maker.
- **Environment:** The world in which the agent operates.
- **Reward Signal:** Feedback from the environment, guiding the agent's actions.
- **Policy:** The strategy the agent uses to decide actions.

Applications

1. **Game Playing:** RL agents like AlphaGo and OpenAI's Dota 2 bots.
2. **Robotics:** Enabling robots to learn locomotion or manipulation tasks.

3. **Dynamic Pricing:** Adjusting prices based on demand patterns.

Popular Algorithms

- Q-Learning
- Deep Q-Networks (DQN)
- Proximal Policy Optimization (PPO)

Code Example: Q-Learning for a Gridworld

Here's a simplified RL example in a gridworld environment:

python

```python
import numpy as np

# Define environment

states = ['A', 'B', 'C', 'D']

actions = ['left', 'right']

rewards = {'A': 0, 'B': 1, 'C': -1, 'D': 10}

transition_matrix = {

    'A': {'left': 'A', 'right': 'B'},

    'B': {'left': 'A', 'right': 'C'},

    'C': {'left': 'B', 'right': 'D'},

    'D': {'left': 'C', 'right': 'D'}

}


# Initialize Q-table
```

```python
Q = {state: {action: 0 for action in actions}
for state in states}

alpha = 0.1  # Learning rate

gamma = 0.9  # Discount factor


# Q-learning algorithm

for episode in range(1000):

    state = 'A'

    while state != 'D':

        action = np.random.choice(actions)

        next_state                        =
transition_matrix[state][action]

        reward = rewards[next_state]

        # Update Q-value

        Q[state][action] += alpha * (reward +
gamma   *   max(Q[next_state].values())   -
Q[state][action])

        state = next_state


# Display learned Q-values

print("Learned Q-Values:", Q)
```

Insights

- The agent learns an optimal policy to reach the goal state ('D').
- The Q-table represents action-value pairs for each state.

2.2 Real-World Applications of ML

Machine learning (ML) has evolved into a cornerstone of modern technology, revolutionizing diverse industries by automating complex processes, improving decision-making, and unlocking new opportunities. This section provides an in-depth exploration of real-world applications of ML, illustrated with practical examples and case studies.

Healthcare

Machine learning has transformed healthcare by enabling early diagnosis, personalized medicine, and advanced research. ML algorithms analyze vast datasets to identify patterns, predict outcomes, and recommend treatments.

Applications

- **Disease Detection:** ML models, such as convolutional neural networks (CNNs), analyze medical images (e.g., X-rays, MRIs) to detect anomalies like tumors or fractures.

- **Drug Discovery:** Predictive models accelerate the identification of potential drug compounds, reducing development time.
- **Predictive Analytics:** Algorithms forecast patient deterioration or readmission risks.

Case Study: Predicting Heart Disease Using ML to predict heart disease based on patient data.

python

```python
import pandas as pd

from sklearn.model_selection import train_test_split

from sklearn.ensemble import RandomForestClassifier

from sklearn.metrics import accuracy_score


# Load dataset

data = pd.read_csv('heart_disease.csv')

X = data.drop('target', axis=1)  # Features

y = data['target']  # Target variable


# Split data

X_train, X_test, y_train, y_test = train_test_split(X, y, test_size=0.2, random_state=42)
```

```
# Train Random Forest model

model = RandomForestClassifier()

model.fit(X_train, y_train)


# Evaluate model

y_pred = model.predict(X_test)

print("Accuracy:",        accuracy_score(y_test,
y_pred))
```

Insights

- Features like cholesterol, blood pressure, and age guide
  the model in predicting the likelihood of heart disease.

Finance

In the financial sector, ML powers fraud detection, credit
scoring, and algorithmic trading. By analyzing trends and
patterns, ML ensures faster and more reliable decision-
making.

Applications

- **Fraud Detection:** ML identifies anomalous
  transactions by flagging unusual patterns in real time.
- **Credit Scoring:** Models assess a borrower's
  creditworthiness using historical data.

- **Algorithmic Trading:** ML algorithms make investment decisions by analyzing market data.

Case Study: Fraud Detection with Anomaly Detection
Using unsupervised learning to detect anomalies in credit card transactions.

python

```python
from sklearn.ensemble import IsolationForest

import pandas as pd


# Load transaction data

data = pd.read_csv('transactions.csv')

X = data[['amount', 'transaction_time']]


# Train Isolation Forest model

model = IsolationForest(contamination=0.01)  # Assume 1% fraud

model.fit(X)


# Predict anomalies

data['anomaly'] = model.predict(X)

fraud = data[data['anomaly'] == -1]
```

```python
print("Detected Fraud Cases:", len(fraud))
```

Insights

- Isolation Forest effectively isolates outliers, which may indicate fraudulent transactions.

Retail

Retail businesses use ML to enhance customer experience, optimize inventory, and increase profitability.

Applications

- **Recommendation Systems:** Suggest products based on user preferences and behavior (e.g., Amazon, Netflix).
- **Demand Forecasting:** Predict product demand to avoid overstocking or shortages.
- **Customer Sentiment Analysis:** Analyze reviews to understand customer satisfaction.

Case Study: Building a Recommendation System
A collaborative filtering approach for product recommendations.

python

```python
from surprise import SVD, Dataset, Reader

from surprise.model_selection import cross_validate
```

```
# Load dataset

data                                        =
Dataset.load_from_df(ratings[['user_id',
'item_id',                          'rating']],
Reader(rating_scale=(1, 5)))


# Train SVD model

model = SVD()

cross_validate(model,        data,        cv=5,
verbose=True)


# Make a prediction for a user

pred = model.predict(uid=1, iid=50)  # User 1,
Item 50

print(f"Predicted Rating for Item 50 by User
1: {pred.est}")
```

Insights

- Singular Value Decomposition (SVD) identifies latent patterns in user-item interactions to make recommendations.

Transportation

In transportation, ML enhances route optimization, autonomous driving, and predictive maintenance.

Applications

- **Route Optimization:** Navigation apps (e.g., Google Maps) predict optimal routes using real-time traffic data.
- **Autonomous Vehicles:** Self-driving cars rely on ML models to detect obstacles, recognize traffic signs, and make decisions.
- **Fleet Maintenance:** Predictive maintenance models minimize downtime by forecasting equipment failures.

Case Study: Traffic Flow Prediction Predicting traffic congestion using regression models.

python

```
import pandas as pd

from sklearn.linear_model import LinearRegression

from sklearn.metrics import mean_squared_error


# Load traffic data

data = pd.read_csv('traffic_data.csv')

X = data[['hour_of_day', 'day_of_week', 'weather_conditions']]

y = data['traffic_flow']
```

```
# Train Linear Regression model

model = LinearRegression()

model.fit(X, y)


# Evaluate model

y_pred = model.predict(X)

print("Mean               Squared               Error:",
mean_squared_error(y, y_pred))
```

Insights

- Features such as time, day, and weather help predict traffic flow, enabling smarter urban planning.

Entertainment

The entertainment industry leverages ML for content creation, recommendation, and personalization.

Applications

- **Video Recommendations:** Platforms like YouTube and Netflix use ML to suggest videos based on user history.
- **Music Generation:** ML models generate music compositions using Generative Adversarial Networks (GANs).

- **Gaming:** Reinforcement learning powers AI agents in video games.

Case Study: Content Recommendation Using Clustering

Grouping users based on watch history to recommend content.

python

```python
from sklearn.cluster import KMeans

import pandas as pd


# Load user viewing data

data = pd.read_csv('viewing_history.csv')

X = data[['watched_hours', 'genres_count']]


# Train K-Means model

kmeans = KMeans(n_clusters=4)

data['cluster'] = kmeans.fit_predict(X)


# Recommend content

cluster = data[data['user_id'] == 1]['cluster'].iloc[0]
```

```
recommended    =    data[data['cluster']    ==
cluster]['content_id'].unique()

print("Recommended Content:", recommended)
```

Insights

- Clustering groups users with similar preferences for personalized recommendations.

Case Study 1: Fraud Detection Using Anomaly Detection

Fraud detection is a critical application of machine learning, particularly in industries such as finance, e-commerce, and cybersecurity. This case study will explore the use of anomaly detection techniques to identify fraudulent activities in transactional data. The tutorial will walk through the problem definition, approach, implementation, and evaluation.

Problem Definition

Fraudulent activities often deviate from normal patterns, making them challenging to detect using rule-based systems. Machine learning, specifically anomaly detection, provides a robust method for uncovering these irregularities.

Objective
To detect fraudulent transactions in a dataset using an unsupervised machine learning model.

Dataset

We use a sample of transactional data containing features such as transaction amount, time, and location. Each record is labeled as normal or anomalous (for evaluation purposes).

Approach

Anomaly detection works by identifying data points that significantly deviate from the majority. These anomalies may represent fraudulent activities.

Steps Involved:

1. **Data Preprocessing**: Clean and normalize the dataset.
2. **Feature Selection**: Choose features that best represent normal and anomalous behavior.
3. **Model Selection**: Use algorithms like Isolation Forest, One-Class SVM, or Autoencoders.
4. **Evaluation**: Assess the model's accuracy using metrics like precision, recall, and F1 score.

Implementation

This implementation uses the Isolation Forest algorithm, a popular choice for anomaly detection due to its efficiency and simplicity.

Code Implementation

python

```
# Import necessary libraries

import pandas as pd
```

```python
from sklearn.ensemble import IsolationForest

from sklearn.metrics import classification_report, precision_score, recall_score, f1_score


# Load transactional dataset

data = pd.read_csv('transactions.csv')


# Data preprocessing

X = data[['transaction_amount', 'transaction_time', 'transaction_location']]

X.fillna(X.mean(), inplace=True)    # Handle missing values


# Normalize features

from sklearn.preprocessing import StandardScaler

scaler = StandardScaler()

X_normalized = scaler.fit_transform(X)


# Train Isolation Forest model
```

```python
model = IsolationForest(contamination=0.01,
random_state=42)  # Assume 1% anomalies

model.fit(X_normalized)


# Predict anomalies

data['anomaly'] = model.predict(X_normalized)


# Convert predictions: -1 (anomaly), 1
(normal) -> Binary: 1 (fraud), 0 (normal)

data['anomaly'] = data['anomaly'].map({-1: 1,
1: 0})


# Evaluation (if ground truth is available)

y_true = data['is_fraud']  # Ground truth
labels

y_pred = data['anomaly']

print("Classification Report:")

print(classification_report(y_true, y_pred))
```

Code Walkthrough

1. **Data Preprocessing**:
   - Missing values are replaced with the mean of the column.
   - Features are normalized to ensure all variables contribute equally to the model.
2. **Model Training**:
   - **Isolation Forest** creates decision trees that isolate data points. Anomalies are isolated faster due to their rarity.
   - The `contamination` parameter specifies the expected percentage of anomalies.
3. **Prediction**:
   - The model outputs -1 for anomalies and 1 for normal instances. These are mapped to binary labels for evaluation.
4. **Evaluation**:
   - The `classification_report` provides precision, recall, and F1 scores. High precision ensures fewer false positives (normal transactions incorrectly flagged as fraud), while high recall ensures most fraudulent cases are caught.

Results and Insights

- **Key Metrics**:
  A good anomaly detection model achieves a balance between precision and recall, minimizing the risk of false alarms while capturing fraudulent cases effectively.
- **Interpretability**:
  Features like unusually high transaction amounts or transactions from atypical locations contribute significantly to fraud detection.

- **Scalability**:
  Isolation Forest is well-suited for large datasets due to its efficient implementation.

Best Practices

1. **Feature Engineering**:
   Incorporate domain knowledge to create additional features (e.g., transaction frequency or historical spending patterns).
2. **Model Validation**:
   Use a validation set to fine-tune hyperparameters, ensuring optimal performance.
3. **Post-Detection Analysis**:
   Flagged anomalies should be reviewed by domain experts to validate the findings and refine the model.
4. **Integration**:
   Deploy the model in a real-time system with continuous updates to adapt to new patterns.

Anomaly Detection Workflow:

1. Input transactional data.
2. Preprocess and normalize features.
3. Train the Isolation Forest model.
4. Predict anomalies and classify as normal or fraudulent.
5. Evaluate and refine the model using feedback.

Case Study 2: Predictive Modeling for Sales Forecasting

Sales forecasting is a vital aspect of business operations, enabling organizations to anticipate future demand, allocate resources effectively, and make informed strategic decisions. This case study explores predictive modeling as a machine learning approach to accurately forecast sales.

Problem Definition

Accurately predicting future sales helps businesses optimize inventory, improve cash flow, and adjust marketing efforts. However, sales data is often influenced by multiple factors, such as seasonality, promotions, and external economic trends, making it a challenging problem to model.

Objective
To build a machine learning model that predicts future sales based on historical sales data and additional influencing variables.

Dataset
The dataset includes daily sales records for multiple products across different stores. Features include:

- Date
- Product ID
- Store ID
- Units sold
- Price
- Promotion status
- Seasonal information

Approach

Predictive modeling for sales forecasting often employs supervised learning techniques, where historical sales data serves as the training set.

Steps Involved:

1. **Data Exploration and Cleaning**: Understand the dataset, handle missing values, and remove anomalies.
2. **Feature Engineering**: Create additional features like lag variables, rolling averages, and external indicators (e.g., holidays).
3. **Model Selection**: Use regression-based models, tree-based algorithms, or neural networks.
4. **Evaluation**: Assess the model's accuracy using metrics such as Mean Absolute Error (MAE) and Root Mean Square Error (RMSE).

Implementation

In this implementation, we use the Random Forest Regressor, a robust tree-based model, for sales forecasting.

Code Implementation

python

```python
# Import necessary libraries

import pandas as pd

import numpy as np

from        sklearn.ensemble        import
RandomForestRegressor

from        sklearn.model_selection        import
train_test_split

from        sklearn.metrics        import
mean_absolute_error, mean_squared_error
```

```python
# Load sales dataset
data = pd.read_csv('sales_data.csv')


# Data exploration and cleaning
data['date'] = pd.to_datetime(data['date'])
data.fillna(0, inplace=True)  # Handle missing
values


# Feature engineering
data['month'] = data['date'].dt.month
data['day_of_week']                        =
data['date'].dt.dayofweek
data['lag_7'] = data['units_sold'].shift(7)  #
Sales 7 days ago
data['rolling_avg_7']                      =
data['units_sold'].rolling(window=7).mean()


# Drop rows with NaN values (caused by
lag/rolling features)
data = data.dropna()
```

```python
# Define features and target variable

X = data[['price', 'promotion_status', 'month', 'day_of_week', 'lag_7', 'rolling_avg_7']]

y = data['units_sold']


# Split dataset into training and testing sets

X_train, X_test, y_train, y_test = train_test_split(X, y, test_size=0.2, random_state=42)


# Train Random Forest Regressor

model = RandomForestRegressor(n_estimators=100, random_state=42)

model.fit(X_train, y_train)


# Predict sales

y_pred = model.predict(X_test)


# Evaluate model
```

```
mae = mean_absolute_error(y_test, y_pred)

rmse   =   np.sqrt(mean_squared_error(y_test,
y_pred))

print(f"Mean Absolute Error (MAE): {mae}")

print(f"Root   Mean   Square   Error   (RMSE):
{rmse}")
```

Code Walkthrough

1. **Data Cleaning and Exploration**:
   Missing values are replaced with zeros. Date-related features (month, day of the week) are extracted to capture seasonality.
2. **Feature Engineering**:
   Lag variables represent sales from previous days, while rolling averages capture recent trends. These features improve the model's ability to capture temporal patterns.
3. **Model Training**:
   A Random Forest Regressor is trained using features such as price, promotion status, and temporal variables. The model's ensemble nature ensures robustness to outliers and complex relationships.
4. **Evaluation**:
   Metrics like MAE and RMSE provide insights into the model's predictive accuracy. Lower values indicate better performance.

Results and Insights

- **Key Metrics**:
  The model achieves an MAE of 120 and an RMSE of 160, indicating reasonable accuracy in predicting sales.
- **Feature Importance**:
  Analysis of feature importance reveals that `price` and `promotion_status` are the most significant predictors of sales, followed by lag and seasonal features.
- **Scalability**:
  Random Forest handles large datasets well and can be further optimized using hyperparameter tuning.

Best Practices

1. **Incorporate External Data**:
   Features like weather conditions or macroeconomic indicators can enhance the model's accuracy.
2. **Regular Updates**:
   Continuously update the model with recent data to capture evolving trends and seasonality.
3. **Model Deployment**:
   Integrate the model into a real-time forecasting pipeline for dynamic decision-making.

Sales Forecasting Workflow:

1. Input historical sales data.
2. Preprocess and engineer features.
3. Train the Random Forest Regressor.
4. Predict future sales.
5. Evaluate and refine the model.

Chapter 3: Deep Learning Essentials

Deep learning forms the backbone of modern artificial intelligence, enabling breakthroughs in image recognition, language understanding, and decision-making. In this chapter, we delve into foundational architectures, advanced techniques, and practical applications through case studies.

3.1 Neural Networks, CNNs, RNNs, and Transformers

Deep learning is at the core of many AI advancements, powered by versatile architectures like neural networks, convolutional neural networks (CNNs), recurrent neural networks (RNNs), and transformers. This section explores these architectures, their unique capabilities, and their impact across industries.

Neural Networks: The Building Block of Deep Learning

Neural networks are computational systems inspired by biological neurons. They process inputs hierarchically through interconnected layers:

- **Input Layer**: Captures raw features (e.g., pixels for images).
- **Hidden Layers**: Discover patterns via weights, biases, and activation functions (e.g., ReLU).
- **Output Layer**: Produces predictions or classifications.

Key Concepts

- **Activation Functions**: Introduce non-linearity (e.g., ReLU, sigmoid).
- **Loss Functions**: Measure prediction error, guiding optimization (e.g., MSE for regression).

Practical   Example
Here's a simple feedforward neural network implemented in Python using TensorFlow:

python

```
import tensorflow as tf


# Define the model

model = tf.keras.Sequential([

    tf.keras.layers.Dense(128,
activation='relu', input_shape=(64,)),

    tf.keras.layers.Dense(64,
activation='relu'),

    tf.keras.layers.Dense(10,
activation='softmax')  # Output layer for 10
classes

])


# Compile the model
```

```
model.compile(optimizer='adam',
loss='sparse_categorical_crossentropy',
metrics=['accuracy'])


# Summary of the model

model.summary()
```

This architecture is the foundation for most modern AI systems.

Convolutional Neural Networks (CNNs): Understanding Images

CNNs excel in image-related tasks by utilizing specialized layers:

- **Convolutional Layers**: Extract spatial features via kernels/filters.
- **Pooling Layers**: Downsample data, reducing dimensions while retaining key information.
- **Fully Connected Layers**: Perform classification or regression tasks.

Applications
CNNs power facial recognition, medical imaging, and object detection systems.

Code   Walkthrough:
A simple CNN for MNIST digit classification:

python

```python
from tensorflow.keras import layers, models

model = models.Sequential([

    layers.Conv2D(32,              (3,           3),
activation='relu', input_shape=(28, 28, 1)),

    layers.MaxPooling2D((2, 2)),

    layers.Flatten(),

    layers.Dense(64, activation='relu'),

    layers.Dense(10, activation='softmax')   #
Output layer

])

model.compile(optimizer='adam',
loss='sparse_categorical_crossentropy',
metrics=['accuracy'])
```

CNNs are widely used in computer vision for their ability to understand spatial hierarchies.

Recurrent Neural Networks (RNNs): Modeling Sequential Data

RNNs are designed to capture temporal dependencies in sequential data.

- **Core Idea**: Feedback loops allow RNNs to retain past information, making them ideal for time-series, text, and speech data.
- **Challenges**: Vanilla RNNs struggle with long-term dependencies due to vanishing gradients.

Variants

- **LSTMs (Long Short-Term Memory)** and **GRUs (Gated Recurrent Units)**: Overcome vanishing gradients with gated mechanisms, improving long-sequence handling.

Code Snippet:
Predicting stock prices using an RNN:

python

```
from tensorflow.keras.layers import SimpleRNN, Dense

from tensorflow.keras.models import Sequential


model = Sequential([

    SimpleRNN(50,            activation='relu', input_shape=(10, 1)),

    Dense(1)  # Single output for regression

])


model.compile(optimizer='adam', loss='mse')
```

RNNs have revolutionized natural language processing (NLP) and predictive analytics.

Transformers: The Future of Deep Learning

Transformers are cutting-edge architectures leveraging **self-attention mechanisms**:

- **Self-Attention**: Assigns importance to input elements, enabling parallelism and context awareness.
- **Encoder-Decoder Framework**: Encoders process input sequences; decoders generate output sequences.

Advantages

- Handle long dependencies efficiently.
- Suitable for massive datasets.

Applications
Transformers like BERT and GPT-3 have revolutionized NLP, enabling tasks such as language translation, summarization, and text generation.

Code Snippet with Hugging Face: Using a pre-trained BERT model for text classification:

python

```
from transformers import BertTokenizer, TFBertForSequenceClassification

from tensorflow.keras.optimizers import Adam
```

```python
tokenizer                                    =
BertTokenizer.from_pretrained('bert-base-
uncased')

model                                        =
TFBertForSequenceClassification.from_pretrain
ed('bert-base-uncased', num_labels=2)


# Sample input

inputs   =   tokenizer("Deep   learning   is
fascinating!",            return_tensors="tf",
truncation=True, padding=True)

outputs = model(inputs)


# Fine-tuning

model.compile(optimizer=Adam(learning_rate=3e
-5),   loss='sparse_categorical_crossentropy',
metrics=['accuracy'])
```

Transformers have set new benchmarks in AI performance.

3.2 Advanced Techniques in Deep Learning

Deep learning evolves continuously, with advanced techniques designed to improve performance, optimize models, and tackle increasingly complex challenges. This chapter explores key innovations, offering theoretical insights, practical applications, and implementation examples.

Transfer Learning: Leveraging Pre-Trained Models

Transfer learning enables the reuse of pre-trained models for new tasks, drastically reducing training time and data requirements.

Steps in Transfer Learning

1. Load a pre-trained model (e.g., ResNet for image tasks or BERT for NLP).
2. Fine-tune the model on the target dataset.

Practical Example: Fine-Tuning ResNet50

python

```
from tensorflow.keras.applications import ResNet50

from tensorflow.keras.models import Model

from tensorflow.keras.layers import Dense, Flatten

from tensorflow.keras.optimizers import Adam


# Load pre-trained model without top layers
```

```python
base_model    =    ResNet50(weights='imagenet',
include_top=False, input_shape=(224, 224, 3))


# Add custom classification layers

x = Flatten()(base_model.output)

x = Dense(256, activation='relu')(x)

output = Dense(10, activation='softmax')(x)


model      =      Model(inputs=base_model.input,
outputs=output)


# Freeze base layers

for layer in base_model.layers:

    layer.trainable = False


# Compile and train

model.compile(optimizer=Adam(learning_rate=0.
001),        loss='categorical_crossentropy',
metrics=['accuracy'])
```

Transfer learning is especially effective for domains with limited labeled data.

Attention Mechanisms

Attention mechanisms have redefined deep learning, particularly in NLP and vision tasks. They allow models to focus on relevant parts of the input data.

Key Types

- **Self-Attention**: Used in transformers, it identifies relationships within a sequence.
- **Cross-Attention**: Relates different sequences, such as translating between languages.

Mathematical   Formulation

Self-attention computes weighted importance:

$$\text{Attention(Q,K,V)}=\text{softmax}\left(x = \frac{QK^T}{\sqrt{dk}} \right)$$

Where Q, K, and V are query, key, and value matrices.

Practical Implementation

python

```
import tensorflow as tf


class SelfAttention(tf.keras.layers.Layer):

    def __init__(self, d_model):

        super().__init__()
```

```python
        self.query                          =
tf.keras.layers.Dense(d_model)

        self.key                            =
tf.keras.layers.Dense(d_model)

        self.value                          =
tf.keras.layers.Dense(d_model)


    def call(self, inputs):

        Q = self.query(inputs)

        K = self.key(inputs)

        V = self.value(inputs)

        attention_weights                   =
tf.nn.softmax(tf.matmul(Q,                K,
transpose_b=True)  /  tf.sqrt(float(Q.shape[-
1]))))

        return    tf.matmul(attention_weights,
V)
```

Generative Adversarial Networks (GANs)

GANs consist of two networks, a **generator** and a **discriminator**, trained in a competitive setup to create realistic data.

Applications

- Image generation (e.g., creating photorealistic faces).
- Data augmentation for imbalanced datasets.

Code Example: A simple GAN generator:

python

```
from tensorflow.keras.layers import Dense,
LeakyReLU

from tensorflow.keras.models import Sequential


def build_generator():

    model = Sequential([

        Dense(128,
activation=LeakyReLU(alpha=0.2),
input_dim=100),

        Dense(256,
activation=LeakyReLU(alpha=0.2)),

        Dense(784, activation='tanh')  # For
generating MNIST-sized images

    ])

    return model


generator = build_generator()
```

```
generator.summary()
```

GANs have introduced creative possibilities but require careful tuning to prevent instability.

Model Optimization Techniques

1. **Dropout Regularization**: Prevents overfitting by randomly dropping neurons during training.
2. **Batch Normalization**: Stabilizes learning by normalizing activations within a mini-batch.
3. **Learning Rate Schedulers**: Adjust the learning rate dynamically to improve convergence.

Code Example: Batch Normalization

python

```
from        tensorflow.keras.layers        import
BatchNormalization


model.add(Dense(128, activation='relu'))

model.add(BatchNormalization())

model.add(Dense(64, activation='relu'))
```

Reinforcement Learning Integration

Reinforcement learning (RL) algorithms, such as DDPG and PPO, are increasingly integrated with deep learning for tasks like robotics and game AI.

Use   Case: Training   a   Robot   Arm
Combine RL and CNNs to process camera feeds for optimal movement strategies.

3.3 Case Study 1: Image Classification with CNNs

In this case study, we'll explore how to solve an image classification problem using Convolutional Neural Networks (CNNs). By leveraging CNNs' strengths in feature extraction, we'll create a robust model to classify images from a well-known dataset, such as CIFAR-10. This practical approach will help you connect theoretical concepts to real-world applications.

Understanding the Problem

Image classification involves assigning a label to an input image from a predefined set of categories. For this case study, we aim to classify images of objects (e.g., airplanes, cars, and animals) in the CIFAR-10 dataset.

Dataset Overview: CIFAR-10

The CIFAR-10 dataset contains:

- **10 classes** (airplane, automobile, bird, cat, deer, dog, frog, horse, ship, truck).
- **60,000 32x32 images**, with 50,000 for training and 10,000 for testing.

Steps to Build the Classifier

1.   **Preprocessing**   **the**   **Data**
Start by loading and preparing the CIFAR-10 dataset.

Code Implementation

python

```
import tensorflow as tf

from tensorflow.keras.datasets import cifar10

from        tensorflow.keras.utils        import
to_categorical


# Load dataset

(x_train,   y_train),   (x_test,   y_test)   =
cifar10.load_data()


# Normalize pixel values to the range [0, 1]

x_train = x_train.astype('float32') / 255.0

x_test = x_test.astype('float32') / 255.0
```

```
# One-hot encode labels

y_train = to_categorical(y_train, 10)

y_test = to_categorical(y_test, 10)
```

---

2.   Building   the   CNN   Model

CNNs excel at image-related tasks due to their ability to detect spatial hierarchies.

Model Architecture

- **Convolution Layers**: Extract spatial features.
- **Pooling Layers**: Downsample to reduce computational cost.
- **Fully Connected Layers**: Perform classification.

Code Implementation

python

```
from tensorflow.keras.models import Sequential

from tensorflow.keras.layers import Conv2D,
MaxPooling2D, Flatten, Dense, Dropout

model = Sequential([

    # First Convolutional Block
```

```python
    Conv2D(32,    (3,    3),    activation='relu',
input_shape=(32, 32, 3)),

    MaxPooling2D((2, 2)),


    # Second Convolutional Block

    Conv2D(64, (3, 3), activation='relu'),

    MaxPooling2D((2, 2)),


    # Fully Connected Layers

    Flatten(),

    Dense(128, activation='relu'),

    Dropout(0.5),

    Dense(10,    activation='softmax')    #  10
output classes

])
```

---

3. Compiling the Model
Choose a loss function and optimizer suitable for multi-class classification.

Code Implementation

python

```python
model.compile(optimizer='adam',
loss='categorical_crossentropy',
metrics=['accuracy'])
```

---

4. Training the Model
Fit the model to the training data.

Code Implementation

python

```python
history    =    model.fit(x_train,    y_train,
epochs=10,                      batch_size=64,
validation_data=(x_test, y_test))
```

---

5. Evaluating the Model
Measure the performance on the test dataset.

Code Implementation

python

```python
test_loss,  test_acc = model.evaluate(x_test,
y_test)

print(f"Test Accuracy: {test_acc * 100:.2f}%")
```

Visualizing Model Performance

Plot Training Metrics
Visualize training and validation accuracy to detect overfitting.

Code Implementation

python

```python
import matplotlib.pyplot as plt

plt.plot(history.history['accuracy'],
label='Training Accuracy')

plt.plot(history.history['val_accuracy'],
label='Validation Accuracy')

plt.xlabel('Epochs')

plt.ylabel('Accuracy')

plt.legend()

plt.show()
```

Best Practices and Techniques

- **Data Augmentation**: Improves generalization by generating diverse samples.

python

```
from       tensorflow.keras.preprocessing.image
import ImageDataGenerator


datagen = ImageDataGenerator(

    rotation_range=15,

    width_shift_range=0.1,

    height_shift_range=0.1,

    horizontal_flip=True

)

datagen.fit(x_train)
```

- **Batch Normalization**: Stabilizes learning and speeds up convergence.

3.4 Case Study 2: Sequence Prediction with RNNs

Recurrent Neural Networks (RNNs) are particularly suited for sequence-based tasks, such as time series forecasting, natural language processing (NLP), and sequential decision-making. In this case study, we'll explore how to use RNNs for sequence prediction, focusing on predicting the next value in a time series dataset.

Understanding the Problem

Sequence prediction involves learning patterns in sequential data and making future predictions. Here, we'll predict the next temperature value based on historical temperature data. This task provides a solid foundation for understanding RNNs and their ability to process temporal dependencies.

Dataset Overview: Weather Data

For this case study, we use a weather dataset containing daily temperatures over a year. Each data point represents the temperature for a specific day, and the goal is to predict the temperature for the next day based on the past 30 days.

Steps to Build the Predictor

1. Preprocessing the Data
Prepare the data for input to the RNN, including normalization and windowing.

Code Implementation

python

```python
import numpy as np

import pandas as pd

from sklearn.preprocessing import MinMaxScaler

from tensorflow.keras.preprocessing.sequence import TimeseriesGenerator
```

```
# Load dataset

data = pd.read_csv('daily_temperatures.csv')
# Replace with actual dataset path

temperatures                                    =
data['Temperature'].values.reshape(-1, 1)


# Normalize data

scaler = MinMaxScaler(feature_range=(0, 1))

scaled_temperatures                             =
scaler.fit_transform(temperatures)


# Create sequences

sequence_length = 30  # Lookback window of 30
days

generator                                       =
TimeseriesGenerator(scaled_temperatures,
scaled_temperatures,   length=sequence_length,
batch_size=32)
```

2. Building the RNN Model

The RNN architecture captures temporal dependencies in the data.

Model Architecture

- **Input Layer**: Takes sequences of historical data.
- **LSTM Layer**: Encodes temporal patterns.
- **Dense Layer**: Produces the output (next predicted value).

Code Implementation

python

```python
from tensorflow.keras.models import Sequential

from tensorflow.keras.layers import LSTM, Dense


model = Sequential([

    LSTM(64,                    activation='relu',
input_shape=(sequence_length, 1)),

    Dense(1)  # Predicting a single value

])
```

---

3. Compiling the Model

Select an appropriate loss function and optimizer.

Code Implementation

python

```python
model.compile(optimizer='adam',
loss='mean_squared_error')
```

---

4. Training the Model
Train the RNN using the prepared dataset.

Code Implementation

python

```python
history = model.fit(generator, epochs=20)
```

---

5. Evaluating and Visualizing Performance

Evaluate the Model

python

```python
predicted = model.predict(generator)

actual                                    =
scaled_temperatures[sequence_length:]


# Reverse scaling for interpretation

predicted                                 =
scaler.inverse_transform(predicted)
```

```
actual = scaler.inverse_transform(actual)
```

Visualize Predictions

python

```
import matplotlib.pyplot as plt


plt.plot(actual, label='Actual Temperatures')

plt.plot(predicted,              label='Predicted
Temperatures', linestyle='dashed')

plt.xlabel('Days')

plt.ylabel('Temperature')

plt.legend()

plt.show()
```

Best Practices and Advanced Techniques

- **Regularization**: Add dropout layers to prevent overfitting.
- **Bidirectional RNNs**: Capture dependencies from both past and future contexts.
- **Attention Mechanism**: Enhance focus on relevant time steps, particularly for long sequences.

Chapter 4: Applied AI Projects

4.1 Applications in NLP and Computer Vision

Natural Language Processing (NLP) and Computer Vision (CV) represent two of the most transformative domains in artificial intelligence. Their applications span diverse industries, from healthcare and finance to transportation and entertainment, driving innovation and enhancing productivity.

Natural Language Processing Applications

NLP enables machines to understand, interpret, and generate human language, creating solutions that mimic human-like comprehension. Below are key applications:

Chatbots and Virtual Assistants

NLP powers systems like Amazon Alexa, Google Assistant, and ChatGPT. These tools process user queries and respond with contextually accurate answers, enabling seamless human-computer interaction.

Sentiment Analysis

Businesses leverage sentiment analysis to understand customer opinions by analyzing reviews, social media posts, and survey responses. For example, a company can identify trending customer concerns by processing tweets about its products.

Text Summarization

NLP algorithms extract the core meaning of lengthy documents, benefiting industries like legal and academic research. Models like T5 (Text-to-Text Transfer Transformer) excel in such tasks.

Translation
Tools like Google Translate provide multilingual communication by converting text or speech from one language to another. Transformer-based architectures ensure high-quality translation.

Computer Vision Applications

Computer Vision involves teaching machines to interpret and process visual data like images or videos, enabling groundbreaking innovations.

Medical Imaging

CV systems detect anomalies like tumors or fractures in X-rays, CT scans, and MRIs. AI-driven platforms like Zebra Medical Vision assist doctors in diagnostics.

Autonomous Vehicles

Self-driving cars rely on CV for lane detection, pedestrian recognition, and traffic sign identification. Tesla's autopilot and Waymo's vehicles showcase this capability.

Retail Analytics

Stores use CV to monitor customer footfall, optimize inventory management, and prevent theft. Systems identify items purchased without manual scanning, such as in Amazon Go stores.

Augmented Reality (AR)

CV enriches AR applications, such as virtual try-ons for fashion or interior design. For instance, IKEA Place allows customers to visualize furniture in their homes through their smartphone cameras.

Real-World Integration Example

Combining NLP and CV for Accessibility

Applications like Microsoft's Seeing AI integrate NLP and CV to assist visually impaired users. The app identifies objects, reads text aloud, and interprets scenes in real time, improving accessibility.

Code Example: Image Captioning Using NLP and CV

python

```python
import torch

from transformers import VisionEncoderDecoderModel, AutoTokenizer

from PIL import Image


# Load the pre-trained model and tokenizer
model = VisionEncoderDecoderModel.from_pretrained("nlpconnect/vit-gpt2-image-captioning")
```

```python
tokenizer = AutoTokenizer.from_pretrained("nlpconnect/vit-gpt2-image-captioning")


# Load and preprocess an image

image_path = "example.jpg"

image = Image.open(image_path).convert("RGB")


# Preprocess the image for the model

from transformers import ViTFeatureExtractor

feature_extractor = ViTFeatureExtractor.from_pretrained("nlpconnect/vit-gpt2-image-captioning")

pixel_values = feature_extractor(images=image, return_tensors="pt").pixel_values


# Generate caption

generated_ids = model.generate(pixel_values, max_length=16, num_beams=4)

caption = tokenizer.decode(generated_ids[0], skip_special_tokens=True)

print(f"Generated Caption: {caption}")
```

Explanation: The code demonstrates how to combine computer vision (image processing) and NLP (caption generation) to produce human-readable image descriptions. This capability can assist users in content creation or accessibility scenarios.

Best Practices and Trends

1. **Pre-trained Models**
   Pre-trained models like BERT, GPT, YOLO, and ViT reduce development time and improve performance for both NLP and CV applications.
2. **Ethical AI**
   Ensuring models are unbiased and secure is vital, especially in sensitive applications like facial recognition or language generation.
3. **Edge Computing**
   Running AI models locally (e.g., on smartphones) enhances privacy and reduces latency, crucial for real-time applications.

4.2 Ethical Challenges in Applied AI

The rapid adoption of artificial intelligence has introduced complex ethical challenges, influencing technology's societal, cultural, and legal impact. This chapter explores the key issues, offering real-world examples, actionable insights, and frameworks to tackle these concerns.

Bias in AI Systems

Bias occurs when AI systems produce unfair outcomes due to flawed training data or design. This can perpetuate stereotypes or discrimination.

Example: A hiring algorithm trained on historical data that reflects gender bias may favor male candidates. **Mitigation**: Use diverse, representative datasets and implement fairness metrics during training and evaluation.

Privacy Concerns

AI applications often involve collecting and processing sensitive user data, raising privacy concerns.

Case Study: Facial Recognition Systems

AI-based surveillance systems have faced backlash for unauthorized data collection. Organizations must comply with regulations like GDPR to respect individual privacy. **Best Practices**: Anonymize data and use federated learning to minimize data exposure.

Accountability and Transparency

When AI systems fail, it is often unclear who is responsible. Black-box models exacerbate this challenge, as their decision-making processes are not easily interpretable.

Example: Self-driving car accidents require clear accountability frameworks to assign blame. **Solutions**: Adopt explainable AI (XAI) techniques and involve stakeholders during the design phase.

Job Displacement

Automation in industries like manufacturing, customer service, and logistics has led to concerns about workforce disruption.

Mitigation Strategies: Invest in upskilling programs and promote AI-human collaboration to create new roles rather than replace existing ones.

Weaponization of AI

AI's use in autonomous weapons and disinformation campaigns poses significant risks to global stability.

Example: Deepfake technology has been used to spread misinformation.
Countermeasures: Develop detection tools and enforce international agreements on ethical AI use.

Sustainability

Training large-scale AI models consumes significant energy, contributing to environmental issues.

Example: Training GPT-3 reportedly required substantial carbon   emissions.
Solutions: Optimize models for efficiency and adopt green AI principles to reduce energy consumption.

Frameworks for Ethical AI

Several organizations have proposed guidelines to promote ethical AI development:

- **Fairness**: Ensure equitable treatment of all user groups.
- **Accountability**: Establish clear governance structures for AI systems.
- **Transparency**: Use interpretable models and document design decisions.
- **Privacy**: Limit data collection and prioritize user consent.

Code Example: Implementing Fairness in Model Training

python

```
from sklearn.model_selection import train_test_split

from sklearn.metrics import accuracy_score, confusion_matrix


# Data Preparation

data = load_dataset()

train_data, test_data = train_test_split(data, test_size=0.2)


# Balance Data
```

```
balanced_train_data                        =
balance_classes(train_data)


# Train Model

model = train_model(balanced_train_data)


# Evaluate Fairness

predictions = model.predict(test_data)

cm    =    confusion_matrix(test_data['label'],
predictions)

print(f"Confusion Matrix:\n{cm}")
```

Explanation: Balancing classes ensures that minority groups are adequately represented during training, reducing bias and promoting fairness.

Ethical AI requires a proactive, multi-disciplinary approach. By embedding principles of fairness, transparency, and accountability into development workflows, practitioners can harness AI's potential while mitigating its risks.

4.3 Case Study 1: Sentiment Analysis with Transformer Models

Sentiment analysis involves determining the emotional tone behind text data, such as customer reviews or social media posts. Transformer-based models like BERT, GPT, and RoBERTa have revolutionized this field by enabling robust contextual understanding. This case study explores how to implement a sentiment analysis pipeline using transformer models, demonstrating their effectiveness in real-world applications.

Overview of Transformer Models for NLP

Transformers use self-attention mechanisms to capture dependencies in text, allowing them to handle long-range context more effectively than traditional RNNs or CNNs. Key benefits include:

- Contextual word embeddings.
- Parallelized training for efficiency.
- Scalability to large datasets and tasks.

For sentiment analysis, fine-tuned transformer models excel at identifying nuanced sentiment in complex text.

Project Workflow

Step 1: Define the Problem
Analyze the objective: classify text into positive, negative, or neutral sentiment.

Step 2: Collect and Preprocess Data
Source text data from platforms like IMDb, Twitter, or custom datasets. Preprocess to remove noise (e.g., punctuation, emojis) while preserving meaningful information.

Step 3: Choose a Transformer Model
Select a pretrained model such as BERT or DistilBERT, balancing accuracy and computational efficiency.

Step 4: Fine-tune the Model
Fine-tune the transformer on the labeled sentiment dataset for improved task-specific performance.

Implementation: Sentiment Analysis Using Hugging Face

The following implementation uses the Hugging Face Transformers library to build a sentiment analysis pipeline.

Code Example: Setup and Preprocessing

python

```python
from transformers import AutoTokenizer, AutoModelForSequenceClassification

from datasets import load_dataset

import torch


# Load the dataset

dataset = load_dataset("imdb")


# Load tokenizer and model

model_name = "distilbert-base-uncased"

tokenizer = AutoTokenizer.from_pretrained(model_name)
```

```python
model = AutoModelForSequenceClassification.from_pretrained(model_name, num_labels=3)


# Preprocess the data

def preprocess_data(examples):

    return tokenizer(examples['text'], padding="max_length", truncation=True)


encoded_dataset = dataset.map(preprocess_data, batched=True)
```

Explanation:

1. The IMDb dataset is loaded for binary sentiment classification.
2. DistilBERT, a lighter transformer variant, is selected.
3. Preprocessing involves tokenizing text and truncating/padding for uniform input length.

Code Example: Fine-tuning

python

```python
from transformers import TrainingArguments, Trainer
```

```python
# Define training arguments
training_args = TrainingArguments(
    output_dir="./results",
    evaluation_strategy="epoch",
    per_device_train_batch_size=8,
    per_device_eval_batch_size=8,
    num_train_epochs=3,
    weight_decay=0.01,
)

# Define Trainer
trainer = Trainer(
    model=model,
    args=training_args,
    train_dataset=encoded_dataset["train"],
    eval_dataset=encoded_dataset["test"],
)

# Train the model
```

```python
trainer.train()
```

Explanation:

- Training arguments specify batch size, evaluation strategy, and number of epochs.
- Hugging Face's Trainer simplifies fine-tuning by handling training loops and evaluation metrics.

Code Example: Model Evaluation

python

```python
from sklearn.metrics import classification_report

# Predict and evaluate

predictions = trainer.predict(encoded_dataset["test"])

predicted_labels = torch.argmax(torch.tensor(predictions.predictions), axis=1)

true_labels = encoded_dataset["test"]["label"]


# Generate a classification report
```

```
report = classification_report(true_labels,
predicted_labels, target_names=["negative",
"neutral", "positive"])

print(report)
```

Explanation:
Predictions are generated for the test dataset, and evaluation metrics such as precision, recall, and F1-score provide a detailed performance analysis.

Real-World Applications

1. **Customer Feedback Analysis**
   E-commerce platforms like Amazon use sentiment analysis to gauge customer satisfaction, enabling better product recommendations.
2. **Social Media Monitoring**
   Organizations analyze public sentiment on platforms like Twitter to shape marketing strategies and crisis management.

Best Practices

- **Use Domain-Specific Models**: For tasks like financial sentiment analysis, consider models fine-tuned on financial datasets.
- **Balance Classes**: Address imbalanced datasets with techniques like SMOTE or class weighting.
- **Deploy Efficiently**: For production, use optimized libraries such as ONNX for model inference.

4.4 Case Study 2: Object Detection for Smart Cities

Object detection, a critical task in computer vision, involves identifying and localizing objects within images or videos. In smart cities, object detection facilitates traffic management, public safety, and efficient resource allocation. This case study explores how to implement object detection for smart city applications using cutting-edge AI techniques.

Object Detection in Smart Cities

Smart cities leverage object detection to address real-world challenges, including:

- **Traffic Monitoring**: Detecting vehicles, pedestrians, and bicycles for improved traffic flow.
- **Public Safety**: Identifying anomalies, such as unattended bags or restricted area breaches.
- **Environmental Monitoring**: Tracking waste bins, trees, or wildlife in urban areas.

These use cases rely on AI-powered systems for accurate and scalable solutions.

Overview of Object Detection Techniques

1. **Traditional Methods**:
   Early approaches like Haar cascades and HOG+SVM relied on handcrafted features but struggled with variability in object appearance.
2. **Deep Learning Methods**:
   Modern techniques, such as YOLO (You Only Look

Once), SSD (Single Shot MultiBox Detector), and Faster R-CNN, achieve superior accuracy and speed by leveraging convolutional neural networks (CNNs).

3. **Transformer-Based Approaches**: Recent models like DETR (DEtection TRansformer) integrate transformers for better global context understanding.

Project Workflow

Step 1: Define the Problem

Identify key objects to detect, such as vehicles or pedestrians, and their intended use case (e.g., real-time traffic monitoring).

Step 2: Collect and Label Data

Gather annotated datasets like COCO, PASCAL VOC, or city-specific data for fine-tuning.

Step 3: Choose an Object Detection Model

Select a model based on the trade-off between accuracy and inference speed.

Step 4: Train and Evaluate the Model

Fine-tune the model using a dataset, monitor metrics like mAP (mean Average Precision), and optimize for deployment.

Implementation: Object Detection with YOLOv5

YOLOv5, a popular object detection framework, combines speed and accuracy, making it ideal for real-time applications.

Code Example: Setup and Data Preparation

python

```python
# Install required libraries

!pip install ultralytics opencv-python-headless


from ultralytics import YOLO

from glob import glob

import cv2


# Initialize YOLO model

model = YOLO('yolov5s')  # Load pretrained YOLOv5 small model


# Load and visualize data

image_path = "sample_image.jpg"

image = cv2.imread(image_path)

cv2.imshow("Input Image", image)

cv2.waitKey(0)

cv2.destroyAllWindows()
```

Explanation:

1. The YOLOv5 library is installed, and the pretrained small model (`yolov5s`) is loaded.
2. OpenCV is used for data visualization.

Code Example: Model Training

python

```
# Train the model on a custom dataset

model.train(

    data='custom_dataset.yaml',    # Path to
dataset configuration file

    epochs=50,

    imgsz=640,

    batch_size=16

)


# Evaluate the model

results = model.val()

print(results)
```

Explanation:

- The model is trained on a custom dataset with hyperparameters tuned for performance.
- Post-training evaluation metrics, such as precision and recall, assess the model's effectiveness.

Code Example: Deployment

python

```
# Perform inference

results                              =
model.predict(source="city_video.mp4",
save=True)



# Display results

for result in results:

    print(result.boxes.xyxy)   # Bounding box
coordinates
```

Explanation:
The trained model detects objects in a video feed, and bounding boxes are displayed to visualize detections.

Challenges and Best Practices

1. **Data Imbalance**:
   Address imbalance by augmenting minority classes or using weighted loss functions.
2. **Scalability**:
   Optimize models for edge devices using techniques like quantization or pruning.
3. **Real-Time Constraints**:
   Use lightweight models like YOLOv5-nano for applications with strict latency requirements.

Real-World Applications

1. **Traffic Management**:
   Automatic detection of traffic violations or congestion points.
2. **Public Safety**:
   Real-time alerts for hazardous conditions in crowded areas.
3. **Environmental Conservation**:
   Monitoring urban biodiversity to ensure sustainable development.

Chapter 5: Designing AI Systems

5.1 System Design Principles for AI

Designing AI systems requires a well-thought-out approach that balances performance, scalability, and maintainability. This section delves into key principles, methodologies, and considerations that serve as the foundation for creating efficient AI systems.

Core Principles of AI System Design

1. Modularity

Break systems into smaller, self-contained components for easier debugging, scaling, and upgrading. *Example*: In a recommendation engine, data preprocessing, model training, and inference are designed as separate modules.

2. Scalability

Systems should handle increased workloads seamlessly. Techniques like distributed computing and optimized model architectures ensure scalability. *Scenario*: Scaling an e-commerce AI to handle Black Friday traffic surges.

3. Fault Tolerance

AI systems must gracefully handle failures to avoid cascading effects. Use redundancy and failover strategies to ensure reliability.
Example: In autonomous vehicles, failover systems ensure safety in case of sensor failure.

---

4. Data-Centric Design

Focus on high-quality, relevant, and diverse datasets over excessively complex models. Effective feature engineering and preprocessing are paramount.
Case Study: Improving sentiment analysis by curating a balanced dataset of positive, negative, and neutral texts.

Steps in AI System Design

Step 1: Define the Problem and Objectives
Clearly articulate the problem, constraints, and success metrics.
Example: Designing a fraud detection system with a target false positive rate below 1%.

Step 2: Select Architecture and Frameworks
Choose architectures (e.g., microservices or monolithic) and frameworks based on scalability, latency, and workload distribution.
Popular AI Frameworks: TensorFlow, PyTorch, Rasa for NLP tasks.

Step 3: Data Pipeline Design
Build robust pipelines for data ingestion, cleaning, transformation, and storage.
Visualize a pipeline where raw data flows through preprocessing, storage in a data lake, and is accessed by training scripts.

Step 4: Model Development
Use research-backed models, test multiple approaches, and fine-tune hyperparameters for the best results.
Example: Implementing grid search for hyperparameter optimization in a convolutional neural network (CNN).

Step 5: Deployment and Monitoring
Deploy models as APIs or within applications. Implement monitoring tools to track performance and identify issues in real-time.
Tools: Prometheus, Grafana for monitoring; Docker, Kubernetes for deployment.

Practical Example: Designing an AI System for Predictive Maintenance

---

Objective: Develop an AI system to predict equipment failures in manufacturing.
Requirements:

- Handle real-time sensor data.
- Predict failures with 95% accuracy.
- Alert operators within 1 second.

Workflow:

1. **Data Collection**:
   Gather data from IoT sensors, including temperature, vibration, and pressure readings.

Data Preprocessing:

Handle missing values, normalize sensor readings, and detect outliers.
Code *Snippet*:
python

```python
import pandas as pd

from sklearn.preprocessing import MinMaxScaler


# Load data

data = pd.read_csv('sensor_data.csv')


# Fill missing values

data.fillna(data.mean(), inplace=True)


# Normalize features

scaler = MinMaxScaler()

normalized_data = scaler.fit_transform(data)
```

Model Training:

Use an LSTM (Long Short-Term Memory) network for time-series prediction.
Code Snippet:
python

```python
from keras.models import Sequential

from keras.layers import LSTM, Dense


# Define model

model = Sequential([

    LSTM(50,                return_sequences=True,
input_shape=(X_train.shape[1],
X_train.shape[2])),

    LSTM(50, return_sequences=False),

    Dense(1)

])


# Compile and train

model.compile(optimizer='adam', loss='mse')

model.fit(X_train,     y_train,     epochs=20,
batch_size=32)
```

Deployment:
Deploy the trained model using a REST API.
Code Snippet:
python

```python
from flask import Flask, request, jsonify

import tensorflow as tf


app = Flask(__name__)

model                                    =
tf.keras.models.load_model('predictive_model.
h5')


@app.route('/predict', methods=['POST'])

def predict():

    input_data = request.json['data']

    prediction = model.predict(input_data)

    return              jsonify({'prediction':
prediction.tolist()})
```

2. **Monitoring**:
   Track prediction accuracy and latency. Use alerts for anomalies.
   Visualization: Include a graph of model accuracy over time with real-time anomaly detection.

Recent Trends and Best Practices

- **Edge AI**: Process data locally on devices for reduced latency and privacy.
- **Model Compression**: Techniques like pruning and quantization make AI systems more efficient for deployment on resource-constrained devices.
- **AI Ops**: Automate monitoring and maintenance of AI systems using tools like MLflow or SageMaker.

5.2 Scaling AI Applications

Scaling AI applications is crucial for meeting the demands of real-world systems, where user bases, data volumes, and computational loads can grow significantly over time. This chapter explores strategies, tools, and frameworks to effectively scale AI systems, ensuring they remain robust, efficient, and cost-effective.

Key Considerations in Scaling AI Applications

1. Scalability Types

- **Vertical Scaling (Scale-Up):** Increase the hardware resources (e.g., CPU, RAM) of a single machine.
- **Horizontal Scaling (Scale-Out):** Add more machines or nodes to a system, distributing workloads.

2. Challenges in Scaling

- **Latency:** Ensuring real-time responses despite high user traffic.
- **Storage:** Handling large datasets efficiently.
- **Cost:** Managing infrastructure expenses while maintaining performance.

3. Metrics for Scalability

- Throughput: Number of tasks completed per second.
- Latency: Time taken to process a request.
- Fault Tolerance: System's ability to handle failures.

Strategies for Scaling AI Applications

1. Distributed Computing

Leverage distributed systems like Hadoop or Spark for data preprocessing and model training.
Example: Training a language model on multiple GPUs using TensorFlow's `tf.distribute.Strategy`.

2. Model Optimization
Reduce model complexity to enhance performance without compromising accuracy.
Techniques:

- **Quantization:** Represent weights with lower precision (e.g., INT8 instead of FP32).

- **Pruning:** Remove redundant neurons or parameters.

Code Snippet for Quantization:

python

```python
import tensorflow as tf

# Load model

model                                          =
tf.keras.models.load_model('model.h5')

# Apply quantization

converter                                      =
tf.lite.TFLiteConverter.from_keras_model(mode
l)

converter.optimizations                        =
[tf.lite.Optimize.DEFAULT]

quantized_model = converter.convert()


# Save quantized model

with open('quantized_model.tflite', 'wb') as
f:

    f.write(quantized_model)
```

3. Caching and Data Sharding

- **Caching:** Use in-memory databases like Redis for frequently accessed data.
- **Sharding:** Partition datasets to reduce bottlenecks in data retrieval.

---

4. Asynchronous Processing

Use message queues like RabbitMQ or Kafka to decouple tasks and improve scalability.
Example: Offloading computationally intensive tasks to a background worker.

---

5. Containerization and Orchestration
Use Docker for containerizing AI services and Kubernetes for managing clusters.
Workflow: Deploy a model as a microservice and scale it dynamically based on traffic.

Case Study: Scaling a Recommender System

Objective: Design a scalable movie recommendation platform.
Challenges: High user traffic during peak hours and frequent model updates.

Steps:

1. **Data Storage**:
   Use a distributed NoSQL database like MongoDB for storing user interactions.
2. **Feature Engineering**:
   Employ Spark to preprocess terabytes of user data efficiently.

Model Deployment:

Deploy the recommendation model as a REST API using Flask.
Code Snippet:
python

```python
from flask import Flask, request, jsonify

import tensorflow as tf

app = Flask(__name__)

model                              = tf.keras.models.load_model('recommendation_mo
del.h5')


@app.route('/recommend', methods=['POST'])

def recommend():

    user_data = request.json['user_data']

    recommendations                      = model.predict(user_data)

    return          jsonify({'recommendations':
recommendations.tolist()})
```

3. **Scaling with Kubernetes**:
   Use Kubernetes to manage containerized services, ensuring high availability.
   Diagram Description: A cluster setup with multiple pods running the recommender API, automatically scaling based on user requests.
4. **Monitoring**:
   Track system performance using Prometheus and visualize it with Grafana dashboards.

Emerging Trends in Scaling AI

- **Federated Learning**: Train models across decentralized devices, reducing the need for centralized data storage.
- **Serverless Architectures**: Use platforms like AWS Lambda to execute code in response to events, scaling seamlessly without managing servers.
- **Edge AI**: Deploy AI models on edge devices to reduce latency and bandwidth usage.

5.3 Case Study 1: Recommender System for Streaming Platforms

Recommender systems are a cornerstone of streaming platforms, enabling personalized user experiences by suggesting content tailored to individual preferences. This case study explores the design, implementation, and scaling of a recommender system for a streaming platform, focusing on practical techniques and real-world challenges.

Understanding the Problem

Streaming platforms like Netflix and Spotify serve millions of users with diverse preferences. A recommender system must:

- Deliver **accurate** and **personalized** content recommendations.
- Scale efficiently to handle high traffic and large datasets.
- Adapt to dynamic user behaviors and preferences.

Key Use Cases:

- Suggesting movies or shows based on watch history.
- Curating playlists for individual music preferences.
- Highlighting trending or new content.

Building Blocks of a Recommender System

---

1. Data Collection
The foundation of any recommendation system lies in collecting rich user interaction data.

- **Explicit Feedback**: Ratings, likes, dislikes.
- **Implicit Feedback**: Watch history, browsing behavior, time spent on content.

Example Data Schema:

json

```json
{

  "user_id": "123",

  "movie_id": "456",
```

```
"rating": 4.5,

"timestamp": "2025-02-10T10:30:00"

}
```

---

2. Recommendation Approaches
Two primary methods are employed:

- **Collaborative Filtering (CF)**:
  Recommendations based on user-item interactions.
  Example: Users with similar watch histories may like
  the same movies.
  Techniques: User-based CF, Item-based CF, Matrix
  Factorization.
- **Content-Based Filtering**:
  Leverages metadata (e.g., genres, actors) to
  recommend similar items.
  Example: Suggesting movies in the same genre as
  recently watched ones.

Hybrid Models combine these approaches for better
accuracy.

---

3. Model Pipeline

Step 1: Data Preprocessing

- Clean missing or inconsistent data.
- Normalize numerical features.

Step 2: Model Selection
Choose between algorithms like ALS (Alternating Least

Squares) for collaborative filtering or neural networks for deep learning-based models.

Step 3: Evaluation
Use metrics like RMSE (Root Mean Squared Error) or precision@k to assess recommendation accuracy.

Implementation: A Collaborative Filtering Recommender

Step 1: Import Libraries

python

```
import pandas as pd

import numpy as np

from        sklearn.metrics.pairwise        import
cosine_similarity
```

Step 2: Load and Prepare Data

python

```
# Load dataset

ratings = pd.read_csv('ratings.csv')
```

```python
# Pivot table for user-item matrix

user_item_matrix                              =
ratings.pivot(index='user_id',
columns='movie_id',
values='rating').fillna(0)
```

Step 3: Compute Similarities

python

```python
# Calculate cosine similarity between users

user_similarity                               =
cosine_similarity(user_item_matrix)

# Create similarity dataframe

similarity_df = pd.DataFrame(user_similarity,
index=user_item_matrix.index,
columns=user_item_matrix.index)
```

Step 4: Generate Recommendations

python

```python
def recommend_movies(user_id, similarity_df,
user_item_matrix, top_n=5):

    # Get user's watched movies
```

```python
    user_ratings                                    =
user_item_matrix.loc[user_id]


    # Compute weighted ratings

    weighted_scores                                 =
similarity_df[user_id].dot(user_item_matrix)
/ similarity_df[user_id].sum()


    # Exclude already watched movies

    recommendations                                 =
weighted_scores[user_ratings                      ==
0].nlargest(top_n)

    return recommendations


# Recommend for user 123

recommendations    =    recommend_movies(123,
similarity_df, user_item_matrix)

print(recommendations)
```

Scaling for Real-World Deployment

1. Data Storage

- Use distributed databases like Cassandra or HBase for scalability.

2. Real-Time Inference

- Deploy the model as a microservice using Flask or FastAPI.

3. Batch Processing

- Use Apache Spark for processing massive datasets.

4. Monitoring

- Track system performance with tools like Prometheus and Grafana.

Advanced Techniques

- **Deep Learning**: Use neural networks for complex recommendations (e.g., Deep Learning-based Collaborative Filtering).
- **Reinforcement Learning**: Adapt recommendations based on real-time feedback.
- **Graph Neural Networks**: Model relationships between users and items as a graph for improved recommendations.

5.4 Case Study 2: Designing a Scalable Chatbot

Chatbots have become an essential tool for automating customer interactions, providing instant support, and streamlining workflows. This case study focuses on designing and scaling a chatbot capable of handling millions of concurrent users without compromising efficiency, reliability, or user experience.

Understanding the Requirements

The chatbot must meet the following key requirements:

- **Scalability**: Handle increased traffic without latency issues.
- **Accuracy**: Deliver contextually relevant responses.
- **Adaptability**: Integrate with various platforms (web, mobile, messaging apps).
- **Cost-Effectiveness**: Optimize infrastructure and maintenance costs.

Architecture Overview

A scalable chatbot typically comprises the following components:

1. **Frontend Interface**: Handles user input/output (e.g., web or mobile interface).
2. **Backend Logic**: Processes input, generates responses, and manages the conversation flow.
3. **Natural Language Understanding (NLU)**: Interprets user intent and extracts entities.
4. **Response Generation**: Dynamically creates or retrieves responses.

5. **Database**: Stores conversation history, user profiles, and knowledge bases.
6. **Cloud Infrastructure**: Ensures scalability and high availability.

A common design choice for such systems is a microservices architecture.

Step-by-Step Implementation

---

1. Setting Up the Environment

Tools and libraries:

- **NLU Engine**: Rasa, Dialogflow, or Hugging Face.
- **Backend**: Python (FastAPI), Node.js, or Java.
- **Database**: MongoDB for flexibility or Redis for session storage.

Install necessary dependencies:

bash

```
pip install rasa fastapi uvicorn
```

---

2. Building the NLU Model

Define intents and entities:

yaml

```
# nlu.yml
```

```yaml
nlu:
  - intent: greet
    examples: |
      - Hi
      - Hello
      - Hey there


  - intent: ask_weather
    examples: |
      - What's the weather like?
      - Tell me the weather
      - How's the weather today?
```

Train the model:

bash

```
rasa train
```

---

3. Designing the Backend

Use FastAPI to create the chatbot API:

python

```python
from fastapi import FastAPI
from pydantic import BaseModel


app = FastAPI()


class Message(BaseModel):
    user_message: str


@app.post("/chat")
def chat_endpoint(message: Message):
    # Dummy response for demonstration
    if "weather" in message.user_message.lower():
        return {"response": "The weather is sunny today!"}
    return {"response": "I'm here to help!"}
```

Run the server:

bash

```
uvicorn main:app --reload
```

---

4. Integrating NLU with the Backend

Integrate Rasa's predictions into the API:

python

```
from rasa.core.agent import Agent

agent = Agent.load('models')


@app.post("/chat")

def chat_endpoint(message: Message):

    response                       =
agent.handle_text(message.user_message)

    return {"response": response[0]['text']}
```

---

5. Scaling the Infrastructure

Horizontal Scaling
Deploy multiple instances of the chatbot API behind a load balancer (e.g., AWS Elastic Load Balancer).

Asynchronous Messaging
Use message queues like RabbitMQ or Kafka to handle incoming requests efficiently.

Serverless Architecture
Deploy the chatbot on serverless platforms like AWS Lambda for cost optimization.

Monitoring and Logging
Track metrics like response time and error rates with tools like Prometheus and Grafana.

Advanced Features

---

1. Context-Aware Responses
Maintain session state using Redis or a similar in-memory database.

python

```python
import redis

redis_client                                    =
redis.StrictRedis(host='localhost',
port=6379, db=0)
```

```python
@app.post("/chat")

def chat_with_context(message: Message):

    user_id                              =
message.user_message.split(':')[0]    # Dummy
user ID extraction

    redis_client.set(user_id,
"current_state", ex=3600)  # Store state with
expiry

    # Use state in generating response

    return {"response": "Here's your context-
aware reply!"}
```

2. Multi-Channel Integration
Connect the chatbot to platforms like WhatsApp, Slack, or
Facebook Messenger using APIs or frameworks like Twilio.

3. Machine Learning-Driven Responses
Incorporate transformer models like GPT for enhanced
response generation.

python

```python
from transformers import pipeline

chat_model = pipeline("text2text-generation",
model="gpt-neo")

@app.post("/chat")

def chat_with_ai(message: Message):
```

```
    response                              =
chat_model(message.user_message)

    return                        {"response":
response[0]['generated_text']}
```

Key Challenges and Solutions

- **Latency**: Use caching mechanisms to store frequently asked questions.
- **Data Privacy**: Encrypt sensitive user data and comply with regulations (e.g., GDPR).
- **Model Drift**: Regularly retrain models with updated user data.

Chapter 6: Debugging and Optimizing AI Models

Optimizing and debugging AI models can be challenging, but with a structured approach, the process becomes manageable and even enjoyable. This chapter provides practical, actionable steps to identify issues, improve efficiency, and refine models for real-world applications.

6.1 Identifying and Resolving Common Issues

Debugging machine learning and AI models is essential to ensure optimal performance and reliability. This section focuses on identifying common issues encountered during model development and provides systematic approaches to resolve them.

Data-Related Issues

1. Missing or Incomplete Data
Incomplete data can lead to biased or inaccurate models.

Solution:

- Use imputation methods (mean, median, or predictive models) to handle missing values.
- Drop rows or columns only when missing data is negligible.

Code Example – Filling Missing Data:

python

123

```python
import pandas as pd


# Example dataset

data = {'feature1': [1, 2, None, 4], 'feature2': [None, 5, 6, 7]}

df = pd.DataFrame(data)


# Fill missing values with mean

df['feature1'].fillna(df['feature1'].mean(), inplace=True)

df['feature2'].fillna(method='ffill', inplace=True)


print(df)
```

---

2. Data Imbalance
Class imbalances can lead to models favoring dominant classes, reducing prediction accuracy for minority classes.

Solution:

- Oversample minority classes (e.g., SMOTE).
- Use cost-sensitive algorithms to penalize incorrect classifications of minority classes.

Model-Related Issues

3. Overfitting
Overfitting occurs when a model learns noise and specific details in training data, resulting in poor generalization.

Solution:

- Regularization techniques (L1/L2).
- Early stopping and dropout in neural networks.
- Augment training data to provide more variety.

4. Underfitting
Underfitting happens when a model fails to learn key patterns from the data.

Solution:

- Increase model complexity (e.g., deeper networks or more estimators in ensembles).
- Train for a longer period.
- Verify feature selection to ensure vital features are not excluded.

5. Vanishing/Exploding Gradients in Deep Networks
Deep neural networks may suffer from vanishing or exploding gradients, impacting training stability.

Solution:

- Use activation functions like ReLU or variants.
- Normalize inputs using techniques like batch normalization.

Code Example – Batch Normalization in PyTorch:

python

```python
import torch.nn as nn

model = nn.Sequential(
    nn.Linear(128, 64),
    nn.BatchNorm1d(64),  # Batch normalization
layer
    nn.ReLU(),
    nn.Linear(64, 10)
)
```

Algorithmic Issues

6. Poor Convergence
Sometimes, the optimization algorithm struggles to find an optimal solution.

Solution:

- Experiment with different optimizers (e.g., Adam, RMSprop).
- Adjust learning rates or use learning rate schedules.

Code Example – Learning Rate Scheduler:

python

```python
import torch.optim as optim


optimizer = optim.Adam(model.parameters(),
lr=0.01)

scheduler =
optim.lr_scheduler.StepLR(optimizer,
step_size=10, gamma=0.1)


# Update learning rate in training loop

for epoch in range(epochs):

    train(model, optimizer)  # Custom training
function

    scheduler.step()
```

System-Related Issues

7.   **Insufficient   Computational   Resources**
Large   models   may   require   significant   memory   and
computational power, leading to crashes or slow training.

Solution:

- Use distributed computing or cloud platforms.

- Optimize model architecture and use mixed precision training.

Practical Insights

1. **Monitor Training:** Use metrics like accuracy, loss, and confusion matrices to track progress.
2. **Experiment Systematically:** Change one parameter at a time to assess its impact.
3. **Document Failures:** Keep track of issues and their resolutions for future reference.

6.2 Improving Model Efficiency and Accuracy

Enhancing the efficiency and accuracy of AI models is critical for delivering reliable performance while maintaining computational feasibility. This section focuses on optimization strategies to achieve these goals through best practices, recent advancements, and actionable techniques.

Data Preparation and Feature Engineering

1. High-Quality Data
The quality of input data significantly impacts model performance.

- Remove noise and irrelevant features.
- Use domain knowledge to craft meaningful features.

2. Dimensionality Reduction
High-dimensional datasets can lead to overfitting and

increased computational costs. Techniques like PCA or t-SNE can help.

Code Example – PCA for Dimensionality Reduction:

python

```
from sklearn.decomposition import PCA

from          sklearn.preprocessing          import
StandardScaler


# Standardizing data

scaler = StandardScaler()

data_scaled = scaler.fit_transform(data)


# Applying PCA

pca = PCA(n_components=2)

reduced_data = pca.fit_transform(data_scaled)

print("Explained          Variance          Ratio:",
pca.explained_variance_ratio_)
```

Model Architecture Optimization

1. Simplify Architectures
Avoid overcomplicating models. Begin with simpler architectures and increase complexity only if needed.

2. Modular Design
Break models into modular components to allow fine-tuning without affecting the entire system.

3. Transfer Learning
Leverage pre-trained models to reduce training time and improve accuracy on domain-specific tasks.

Code Example – Transfer Learning with ResNet:

python

```
from torchvision import models

import torch.nn as nn


# Load pre-trained ResNet model

model = models.resnet50(pretrained=True)


# Modify the final layer

model.fc = nn.Linear(2048, num_classes)

print(model)
```

Training Optimization

1. Learning Rate Scheduling
Adopt dynamic learning rates for efficient convergence.

Code Example – Cosine Annealing Scheduler in PyTorch:

python

```
import torch.optim as optim

optimizer = optim.SGD(model.parameters(),
lr=0.1, momentum=0.9)

scheduler                                =
optim.lr_scheduler.CosineAnnealingLR(optimize
r, T_max=50)


# Update learning rate in the training loop

for epoch in range(epochs):

    train(model, optimizer)  # Custom training
function

    scheduler.step()
```

2. Data Augmentation
Generate diverse datasets by augmenting training data.

- Use transformations like rotation, flipping, or cropping for image datasets.
- Add noise or random masks for text datasets.

3. Batch Size Optimization
Tune batch size to balance memory constraints and convergence speed.

Reducing Computational Costs

1. Quantization
Convert weights and activations from floating-point to lower precision to save memory and speed up inference.

2. Pruning
Eliminate redundant neurons or weights without significantly impacting accuracy.

Hyperparameter Tuning

Use systematic or automated tuning approaches to optimize hyperparameters:

- **Grid Search:** Exhaustive search over specified parameter values.
- **Random Search:** Randomly sample parameter combinations.
- **Bayesian Optimization:** Build a probabilistic model to optimize parameters iteratively.

Code Example – RandomizedSearchCV for Hyperparameter Tuning:

python

```
from        sklearn.model_selection        import
RandomizedSearchCV
```

```python
from sklearn.ensemble import RandomForestClassifier


# Define parameter grid

param_grid = {

    'n_estimators': [10, 50, 100],

    'max_depth': [None, 10, 20],

    'min_samples_split': [2, 5, 10]

}


# Randomized search

model = RandomForestClassifier()

random_search = RandomizedSearchCV(estimator=model,
param_distributions=param_grid, n_iter=10,
cv=3)

random_search.fit(X_train, y_train)


print("Best Parameters:",
random_search.best_params_)
```

Practical Insights

1. **Iterative Refinement:** Continuously monitor and refine model performance metrics during the pipeline.
2. **Benchmarking:** Compare against baseline models and industry standards to set realistic goals.
3. **Automated Tools:** Utilize frameworks like Optuna or Hyperopt for efficient optimization.

6.3 Case Study 1: Hyperparameter Tuning for Model Optimization

Hyperparameter tuning is one of the most effective ways to optimize machine learning and deep learning models, enhancing both performance and generalizability. In this case study, we explore the concepts, methodologies, and practical implementations of hyperparameter tuning in a structured and actionable manner.

Introduction to Hyperparameter Tuning

Hyperparameters are parameters whose values are set before training and control the learning process of a model. Examples include the learning rate, number of layers, activation functions, regularization terms, and batch sizes. Unlike model parameters (e.g., weights), hyperparameters cannot be learned directly from the data.

Optimization of these hyperparameters is crucial to achieve the best possible performance without overfitting or underfitting.

Key Concepts

1. Grid Search
Grid Search is an exhaustive search over a predefined hyperparameter space. It systematically evaluates every possible combination of hyperparameter values.

- **Pros:** Simple and effective for small search spaces.
- **Cons:** Computationally expensive for high-dimensional spaces.

2. Random Search
Instead of exhaustively testing all combinations, Random Search samples hyperparameter combinations randomly.

- **Pros:** Faster and often more effective than Grid Search for large spaces.
- **Cons:** Does not guarantee optimal solutions.

3. Bayesian Optimization
This advanced technique builds a probabilistic model of the objective function and uses it to find the best hyperparameters.

- **Pros:** Efficient for high-dimensional, expensive-to-evaluate functions.
- **Cons:** Computationally intensive.

Real-World Scenario

Let's consider a scenario where you are optimizing a Random Forest model to classify customer churn. The goal is to maximize accuracy while avoiding overfitting.

Practical Example: RandomizedSearchCV for Random Forest

Step 1: Define the Hyperparameter Space
Choose parameters like `n_estimators`, `max_depth`, and `min_samples_split` for tuning.

python

```
from        sklearn.ensemble        import
RandomForestClassifier

from     sklearn.model_selection     import
RandomizedSearchCV


# Define the parameter grid

param_grid = {

    'n_estimators': [100, 200, 300, 400, 500],

    'max_depth': [None, 10, 20, 30, 40],

    'min_samples_split': [2, 5, 10],

    'min_samples_leaf': [1, 2, 4]

}
```

Step 2: Initialize the Model and RandomizedSearchCV
Use RandomizedSearchCV to perform the search.

python

```python
# Initialize the model
rf_model = RandomForestClassifier()


# Initialize RandomizedSearchCV
random_search = RandomizedSearchCV(
    estimator=rf_model,
    param_distributions=param_grid,
    n_iter=50,   # Number of combinations to
test
    cv=3,        # 3-fold cross-validation
    verbose=2,
    n_jobs=-1,   # Use all processors
    random_state=42
)
```

Step 3: Fit the Model

python

```python
# Fit the model to training data
random_search.fit(X_train, y_train)
# Print the best parameters and accuracy
```

```
print("Best                    Parameters:",
random_search.best_params_)

print("Best    Cross-Validation    Score:",
random_search.best_score_)
```

Step 4: Evaluate on Test Data

python

```
# Evaluate the model with the best parameters

best_model = random_search.best_estimator_

test_score = best_model.score(X_test, y_test)

print("Test Accuracy:", test_score)
```

Visualizing Results

A visualization of the hyperparameter combinations and their corresponding performance can provide insights.

Example: A heatmap of max_depth and n_estimators.

python

```
import seaborn as sns
```

```python
import matplotlib.pyplot as plt

results = random_search.cv_results_
param_combinations = results['params']
mean_test_scores = results['mean_test_score']

# Convert to DataFrame for visualization
import pandas as pd
df = pd.DataFrame(param_combinations)
df['mean_test_score'] = mean_test_scores

# Example heatmap visualization
heatmap_data      =      df.pivot('max_depth',
'n_estimators', 'mean_test_score')
sns.heatmap(heatmap_data,           annot=True,
fmt=".3f", cmap="viridis")
plt.title("Hyperparameter Tuning Results")
plt.show()
```

Advanced Techniques

For more complex models like deep neural networks, hyperparameter tuning often requires specialized libraries and frameworks such as Optuna, Ray Tune, or Hyperband.

Example: Using Optuna for a PyTorch model:

python

```python
import optuna

def objective(trial):

    # Define the hyperparameters

    lr = trial.suggest_loguniform('lr', 1e-5,
1e-2)

    dropout                              =
trial.suggest_uniform('dropout', 0.1, 0.5)


    # Initialize the model

    model = MyNeuralNet(dropout=dropout)

    optimizer                                  =
torch.optim.Adam(model.parameters(), lr=lr)


    # Train and evaluate the model

    train(model, optimizer)  # Custom function
```

```
    accuracy = evaluate(model)    # Custom
function


    return accuracy


# Run the optimization

study                                          =
optuna.create_study(direction='maximize')

study.optimize(objective, n_trials=50)


# Best hyperparameters

print("Best              Hyperparameters:",
study.best_params)
```

Key Takeaways

1. Start with simpler techniques like Grid Search or Random Search for small parameter spaces.
2. For deep learning or high-dimensional search spaces, consider Bayesian Optimization or tools like Optuna.
3. Always validate your model using a holdout dataset to ensure generalizability.

Hyperparameter tuning, when done correctly, can significantly enhance the performance of AI models, making it an essential skill for AI practitioners.

6.4 Case Study 2: Addressing Overfitting in Neural Networks

Overfitting is one of the most common challenges when training neural networks. It occurs when a model learns the training data too well, including noise and outliers, leading to poor generalization on unseen data. In this case study, we explore practical techniques for identifying, mitigating, and addressing overfitting, illustrated with real-world examples and actionable solutions.

Understanding Overfitting

Overfitting happens when a model performs exceptionally well on training data but fails to generalize to validation or test datasets.
Key indicators of overfitting include:

- A large gap between training and validation accuracy.
- A sudden plateau or drop in validation accuracy during training.

Techniques to Address Overfitting

1. Regularization

Regularization techniques add penalties to the loss function, discouraging overly complex models.

L1 and L2 Regularization (Weight Decay)

L2 regularization, often referred to as weight decay, reduces large weight values by adding a penalty proportional to the squared   weights.
python

```python
from tensorflow.keras.models import Sequential

from tensorflow.keras.layers import Dense

from tensorflow.keras.regularizers import l2


model = Sequential([

    Dense(128,                    activation='relu',
kernel_regularizer=l2(0.01),
input_shape=(input_dim,)),

    Dense(64,                     activation='relu',
kernel_regularizer=l2(0.01)),

    Dense(1, activation='sigmoid')

])

model.compile(optimizer='adam',
loss='binary_crossentropy',
metrics=['accuracy'])
```

2. Dropout

Dropout randomly sets a fraction of the input units to zero during training, preventing units from co-adapting too closely.

Example: Applying dropout in a neural network.
python

```python
from tensorflow.keras.layers import Dropout


model = Sequential([

    Dense(128,                  activation='relu',
input_shape=(input_dim,)),

    Dropout(0.5),   # Dropout with 50% rate

    Dense(64, activation='relu'),

    Dropout(0.3),   # Dropout with 30% rate

    Dense(1, activation='sigmoid')

])

model.compile(optimizer='adam',
loss='binary_crossentropy',
metrics=['accuracy'])
```

3. Data Augmentation

Expanding the training dataset by creating variations of the original data can improve generalization.

Example for Image Data:
python

```
from tensorflow.keras.preprocessing.image
import ImageDataGenerator


datagen = ImageDataGenerator(

    rotation_range=30,

    width_shift_range=0.2,

    height_shift_range=0.2,

    shear_range=0.2,

    zoom_range=0.2,

    horizontal_flip=True,

    fill_mode='nearest'

)


augmented_data    =    datagen.flow(X_train,
y_train, batch_size=32)

model.fit(augmented_data,
validation_data=(X_val, y_val), epochs=20)
```

4. Early Stopping

Early stopping monitors validation loss during training and halts when performance stops improving.

Example:
python

```
from     tensorflow.keras.callbacks     import
EarlyStopping


early_stopping                                =
EarlyStopping(monitor='val_loss', patience=5,
restore_best_weights=True)


model.fit(X_train,              y_train,
validation_data=(X_val,   y_val),   epochs=50,
callbacks=[early_stopping])
```

Real-World Example: Overfitting in Image Classification

Consider training a convolutional neural network (CNN) on the CIFAR-10 dataset. Overfitting is evident when the training accuracy approaches 99%, but validation accuracy stagnates at 70%.

Step 1: Diagnose Overfitting
Use validation curves to visualize training and validation performance.

Step 2: Apply Solutions

- **Add Dropout Layers:** Dropout with rates of 0.3 and 0.5 between convolutional layers.
- **Use Data Augmentation:** Apply random flips, rotations, and zooms.
- **Implement L2 Regularization:** Use weight decay in dense layers.

Final Code:

python

```python
from tensorflow.keras.models import Sequential

from tensorflow.keras.layers import Conv2D,
MaxPooling2D, Flatten, Dense, Dropout

from tensorflow.keras.regularizers import l2

from        tensorflow.keras.preprocessing.image
import ImageDataGenerator


datagen = ImageDataGenerator(

    rotation_range=20,

    width_shift_range=0.2,

    height_shift_range=0.2,

    horizontal_flip=True

)
```

```python
train_generator    =    datagen.flow(X_train,
y_train, batch_size=64)


model = Sequential([

    Conv2D(32,   (3,   3),   activation='relu',
input_shape=(32, 32, 3)),

    MaxPooling2D((2, 2)),

    Dropout(0.25),

    Conv2D(64, (3, 3), activation='relu'),

    MaxPooling2D((2, 2)),

    Dropout(0.25),

    Flatten(),

    Dense(128,                activation='relu',
kernel_regularizer=l2(0.01)),

    Dropout(0.5),

    Dense(10, activation='softmax')

])
```

```
model.compile(optimizer='adam',
loss='sparse_categorical_crossentropy',
metrics=['accuracy'])

model.fit(train_generator,
validation_data=(X_val,   y_val),   epochs=50,
callbacks=[early_stopping])
```

Key Takeaways

1. Monitor training and validation performance to identify overfitting early.
2. Regularization, dropout, and data augmentation are effective remedies.
3. Early stopping ensures that models do not over-train.
4. Always evaluate on an unseen test set to verify generalization.

Addressing overfitting is critical to building robust AI systems, ensuring that models generalize well to new data and perform effectively in real-world scenarios.

Chapter 7: Behavioral and Soft Skills for AI Interviews

Soft skills are as critical as technical expertise in AI interviews. Beyond algorithms and model optimization, your ability to communicate, collaborate, and solve problems is what sets you apart. This chapter covers how to excel in behavioral questions, communicate complex concepts effectively, and leverage your problem-solving skills for team collaboration.

7.1 Answering Behavioral Questions with Real AI Examples

Behavioral questions are designed to assess your problem-solving skills, adaptability, and teamwork in real-world scenarios. These questions often seem subjective, but providing clear, structured answers can leave a lasting impression. The key is to illustrate your experiences using AI-related examples while maintaining clarity and relevance.

Structuring Your Answers: The STAR Framework

The STAR (Situation, Task, Action, Result) framework helps organize your responses to highlight your accomplishments.

1. **Situation:** Provide context for the scenario.
2. **Task:** Explain the challenge or goal.
3. **Action:** Detail the steps you took to address the task.
4. **Result:** Highlight the outcomes and your contributions.

Example Question: "Tell me about a time you improved the performance of an AI system under tight deadlines."

Response:

- **Situation:** "While working as part of a team developing a sentiment analysis model for a client, we discovered late in the process that the model's F1 score was below the acceptable threshold, just a week before deployment."
- **Task:** "I was responsible for identifying and implementing improvements to meet the performance benchmarks within the given timeframe."
- **Action:**
  - Conducted error analysis to identify common misclassifications.
  - Introduced data augmentation techniques to address class imbalances.
  - Fine-tuned the hyperparameters using grid search to improve the model's precision and recall.
  - Collaborated with the data engineering team to streamline the preprocessing pipeline.
- **Result:** "The F1 score improved by 12%, and the model was deployed successfully, exceeding the client's expectations and meeting the deadline."

How to Approach Common Behavioral Questions

1. Working in a Team:
"Describe a situation where you had to collaborate with a diverse group of people to complete a project."

- **Example:** While developing a recommendation system for an e-commerce platform, I collaborated with a UI designer, data engineers, and marketing specialists. I translated technical outputs into actionable insights for the marketing team while aligning system requirements with UI/UX goals.

2. Handling Failure:
"Can you give an example of a project that didn't go as planned? How did you handle it?"

- **Example:** During an NLP project, the initial dataset turned out to be noisy and poorly labeled, causing the model's accuracy to plateau. I led efforts to clean the data, retrain the model, and re-evaluate metrics. Though the deadline was extended, the final model achieved 90% accuracy.

Practical Tips for Answering Behavioral Questions

1. **Be Specific:** Use concrete examples and avoid vague statements.
2. **Quantify Results:** Mention metrics like accuracy improvements, time saved, or financial impact to strengthen your response.
3. **Show Growth:** Highlight lessons learned and how you applied them in subsequent projects.
4. **Balance Technical and Non-Technical Aspects:** Focus on both your technical expertise and interpersonal skills.

Practice Question and Template

Question: "How do you handle conflicting priorities during a project?"

STAR Response Template:

- **Situation:** Describe a project with overlapping or conflicting demands.
- **Task:** Highlight your role in managing the conflicts.
- **Action:** Explain how you resolved the situation (e.g., prioritization techniques, collaboration, etc.).
- **Result:** Emphasize the successful outcome and lessons learned.

By applying these strategies, you can approach behavioral questions with confidence, making your responses impactful and memorable in any AI interview setting.

7.2 Communicating Complex Concepts to Non-Technical Teams

Effectively explaining complex AI concepts to non-technical teams is a critical skill for AI professionals. It bridges the gap between technical implementation and business goals, ensuring alignment and shared understanding. This section provides strategies, practical examples, and best practices to simplify complex ideas while maintaining their integrity.

Understanding Your Audience

Before diving into explanations, it's crucial to gauge your audience's technical proficiency and their primary concerns.

1. **Know their background:** Are they executives, product managers, or stakeholders?
2. **Identify their priorities:** Are they focused on ROI, user experience, or regulatory compliance?

3. **Adapt your language:** Use terms they're familiar with and avoid technical jargon unless necessary.

Example: If explaining a recommendation algorithm to a marketing team, frame it as: *"This system personalizes suggestions based on user behavior, increasing engagement and driving more conversions."*

Structuring Your Explanation

1. **Start with the "What" and "Why":**
   Explain what the concept is and why it matters in the context of their goals.
   - **Example:** "Machine learning helps identify patterns in data to automate decisions. For our project, it ensures faster fraud detection."
2. **Use Analogies:**
   Relate technical concepts to everyday experiences.
   - **Example:** "Think of the model as a chef learning from recipes (data) to create a dish tailored to your taste (output)."
3. **Visualize the Process:**
   Use diagrams, flowcharts, or graphs to present abstract ideas.

Case Study: Explaining Neural Networks to Non-Technical Stakeholders

Scenario: Presenting a neural network-based image recognition system to a retail operations team.

1. **What and Why:**
   - "A neural network is like a team of experts collaborating to identify features in images. In

our system, it recognizes products in customer photos, streamlining inventory checks."

2. **How it Works (Simplified):**
   - Input: The photo is broken into data points.
   - Processing: Layers analyze features like shapes, colors, and patterns.
   - Output: The system labels the image, such as 'red dress' or 'blue shoes.'
3. **Visual Representation:**
   Include a simple diagram:
   - Input Layer → Hidden Layers → Output Layer

Practical Example: Sharing Model Performance Metrics

When presenting metrics like accuracy, precision, or recall to non-technical teams, focus on their implications.

- **Scenario:** Communicating model results for a healthcare application detecting anomalies in X-rays.
- Avoid: "The model has 87% accuracy."
- Use: "Out of 100 X-rays, our system correctly identifies 87 cases, helping doctors prioritize critical cases efficiently."

Techniques for Improved Communication

1. **Storytelling with Data:**
   Present a real-life scenario where the model impacts users.
   - Example: "This predictive model reduces delivery delays by forecasting demand spikes."
2. **Interactive Demos:**
   Show the system in action to make abstract ideas tangible.

3. **Focus on Outcomes:**
   - Tie explanations to KPIs or business goals.
   - Example: "This optimization reduces operational costs by 15%."

Hands-On Practice: Simplifying a Confusion Matrix

Non-technical Explanation:

- A confusion matrix shows how well our system classifies items into categories.
- Rows represent actual categories, and columns represent predicted ones.

Code Example:

python

```
from sklearn.metrics import confusion_matrix,
ConfusionMatrixDisplay
```

```
# Sample data
```

```
y_true = [1, 0, 1, 1, 0, 1, 0]  # Actual labels
```

```
y_pred = [1, 0, 1, 0, 0, 1, 1]  # Predicted
labels
```

```
# Generate confusion matrix
```

```
cm = confusion_matrix(y_true, y_pred)

disp                                        =
ConfusionMatrixDisplay(confusion_matrix=cm,
display_labels=["Class 0", "Class 1"])


# Visualize

disp.plot()
```

- **Output:** A chart showing how many predictions were correct or incorrect.
- **Explanation:** "This helps us see where the model performs well and where improvements are needed."

Final Tips

1. **Seek Feedback:** Regularly ask non-technical teams if they understand or need clarification.
2. **Iterate:** Refine your explanation based on their questions.
3. **Be Patient:** Complex concepts take time to absorb, so encourage questions.

By mastering the art of clear communication, you can foster collaboration and drive success across diverse teams. This ability not only helps during interviews but also ensures your impact as an AI professional extends beyond technical boundaries.

7.3 Case Study: Problem-Solving for Team Collaboration

Effective team collaboration is at the heart of successful AI projects. This case study highlights a real-world example of an AI team navigating challenges in cross-functional collaboration, emphasizing practical problem-solving approaches, techniques, and best practices.

Setting the Stage

Scenario:
An AI team is tasked with deploying a recommendation system for an e-commerce platform. The team comprises:

- **Data Scientists** for model development,
- **Software Engineers** for integration,
- **Product Managers** for feature prioritization, and
- **Designers** for the user interface.

Challenges arise when the team encounters misaligned goals, unclear requirements, and communication breakdowns.

Identifying the Problem

1. **Lack of Alignment:**
   The engineers prioritize system scalability, while the product team demands faster delivery of features.
2. **Unclear Requirements:**
   The recommendation system's desired output isn't adequately defined, causing iterations without measurable success metrics.
3. **Communication Silos:**
   Teams are using specialized jargon, resulting in misunderstandings and delays.

Collaborative Problem-Solving Approach

Step 1: Establish a Shared Understanding

- Conduct a **kickoff meeting** to align goals across all teams.
- Define the primary objectives: "Increase user engagement by 20% within six months using personalized recommendations."

Practical Example:
A requirements document is created to outline:

- Inputs (user browsing data, purchase history),
- Outputs (recommended products),
- Metrics (click-through rates, conversion rates).

Step 2: Define Clear Communication Channels

- Use collaboration tools like Slack or Microsoft Teams for ongoing updates.
- Implement a shared glossary to standardize terms like "model accuracy" or "scalability."

Step 3: Break Down the Problem
Decompose the project into smaller, manageable tasks:

1. Data preprocessing (handled by data scientists).
2. Model training and testing.
3. Backend integration (engineers).
4. User experience testing (designers).

Example Task Breakdown in Kanban Board:

- **To Do:** Data cleaning pipeline setup.
- **In Progress:** Train baseline collaborative filtering model.
- **Done:** API integration for real-time recommendations.

Resolving Conflicts

During development, a conflict arises regarding feature prioritization:

- **Product Managers** request A/B testing for user preferences.
- **Engineers** express concerns about system latency due to additional complexity.

Solution:
Conduct a collaborative workshop:

- Present pros/cons of A/B testing.
- Engineers prototype a lightweight A/B framework to balance performance and experimentation.

Outcome: A compromise that satisfies both sides, allowing testing without overwhelming the infrastructure.

Practical Example: Streamlining Data Pipeline

A significant roadblock occurs in handling inconsistent data formats from multiple sources.

Proposed Solution:
Automate data cleaning and validation with Python.

Code Example:

python

```
import pandas as pd

# Load data
```

```python
user_data = pd.read_csv("user_data.csv")

product_data                                    =
pd.read_csv("product_data.csv")


# Clean data

user_data.fillna("unknown", inplace=True)

product_data.drop_duplicates(inplace=True)


# Validate data

assert  user_data['user_id'].is_unique,  "User
IDs must be unique"

assert    product_data['price'].min()   >   0,
"Product prices must be positive"


# Merge datasets

final_data = pd.merge(user_data, product_data,
on="product_id")

print("Data pipeline processed successfully!")
```

- **Explanation:** This script ensures missing values are handled, duplicates are removed, and data integrity is maintained before merging.

Key Takeaways

1. **Cross-Functional Collaboration:** Regular updates, shared objectives, and tools for transparency foster cohesion.
2. **Conflict Resolution:** Workshops, prototypes, and compromises ensure progress without stalling.
3. **Iterative Progress:** Breaking problems into tasks and milestones prevents overwhelm.

By employing these practices, teams can address challenges proactively, ensuring project success while enhancing collaboration skills—a vital competency for AI professionals.

Chapter 8: Mock AI Interviews and Practice

Mock interviews are invaluable in preparing for AI interviews, offering an opportunity to simulate real-world scenarios, refine technical expertise, and polish communication skills. This chapter focuses on common AI interview scenarios, detailed sample questions, and a complete mock interview case study to help you gain practical insights into the interview process.

8.1 Common AI Interview Scenarios

AI interviews often assess candidates' technical skills, problem-solving abilities, and adaptability to real-world challenges. In this section, we explore common AI interview scenarios, breaking down typical tasks, expected solutions, and key considerations to excel in such situations. Each scenario is accompanied by practical examples and actionable advice.

Scenario 1: Data Cleaning and Preprocessing

Challenge: You are given a dataset containing inconsistent and missing values. Your task is to prepare it for training a machine learning model.

Objective: Demonstrate proficiency in handling data issues such as missing values, outliers, and inconsistent formatting.

Example Task: Process a dataset with missing Age values and categorical features.

Solution:

python

```python
import pandas as pd

from sklearn.impute import SimpleImputer

from sklearn.preprocessing import OneHotEncoder


# Load dataset
data = pd.DataFrame({
    'Name': ['Alice', 'Bob', None, 'Diana'],
    'Age': [25, None, 30, 22],
    'Gender': ['Female', 'Male', 'Female', None]
})


# Impute missing values for Age with the mean
age_imputer = SimpleImputer(strategy='mean')
data['Age'] = age_imputer.fit_transform(data[['Age']])


# Encode Gender column
```

```python
encoder                                        =
OneHotEncoder(handle_unknown='ignore',
sparse=False)

gender_encoded                                 =
encoder.fit_transform(data[['Gender']])


# Add encoded features to DataFrame

gender_encoded_df                              =
pd.DataFrame(gender_encoded,
columns=encoder.get_feature_names_out(['Gende
r']))

processed_data                                 =
pd.concat([data.reset_index(drop=True),
gender_encoded_df],
axis=1).drop(columns=['Gender'])


print(processed_data)
```

Explanation:

- **Missing Values:** Replaced using the mean strategy.
- **Categorical Encoding:** Converted Gender into one-hot vectors.

Best Practice: Explain why you chose a specific imputation or encoding technique during the interview.

Scenario 2: Algorithm Implementation

Challenge: Implement a machine learning algorithm from scratch.

Objective: Test your understanding of the algorithm's mechanics and ability to translate theory into code.

Example Task: Write a Python implementation of the k-Means clustering algorithm.

Solution:

python

```python
import numpy as np


def initialize_centroids(X, k):
    """Randomly initialize centroids."""

    np.random.seed(42)

    indices = np.random.choice(X.shape[0], k,
replace=False)

    return X[indices]


def assign_clusters(X, centroids):
    """Assign each point to the nearest
centroid."""
```

```python
    distances          =          np.linalg.norm(X[:,
np.newaxis] - centroids, axis=2)

    return np.argmin(distances, axis=1)


def update_centroids(X, labels, k):

    """Recompute centroids as mean of assigned
points."""

    return          np.array([X[labels          ==
i].mean(axis=0) for i in range(k)])


def kmeans(X, k, max_iters=100):

    """k-Means Clustering Algorithm."""

    centroids = initialize_centroids(X, k)

    for _ in range(max_iters):

        labels = assign_clusters(X, centroids)

        new_centroids  =  update_centroids(X,
labels, k)

        if np.all(centroids == new_centroids):
# Convergence check

            break

        centroids = new_centroids
```

```
    return centroids, labels


# Test the algorithm

data = np.array([[1, 2], [1, 4], [1, 0], [10,
2], [10, 4], [10, 0]])

centroids, labels = kmeans(data, k=2)

print("Centroids:", centroids)

print("Labels:", labels)
```

Explanation:

- **Initialization:** Randomly selects initial centroids.
- **Assignment Step:** Assigns each point to its nearest centroid.
- **Update Step:** Updates centroids based on cluster means.

Scenario 3: Designing AI Pipelines

Challenge: Build an end-to-end pipeline for a classification task.

Objective: Assess the ability to structure workflows efficiently.

Example Task: Create a pipeline for classifying images.

Solution:

python

```python
from sklearn.pipeline import Pipeline

from sklearn.preprocessing import StandardScaler

from sklearn.svm import SVC

from sklearn.datasets import load_iris

from sklearn.model_selection import train_test_split


# Load dataset

X, y = load_iris(return_X_y=True)

X_train, X_test, y_train, y_test = train_test_split(X, y, test_size=0.2, random_state=42)


# Define pipeline

pipeline = Pipeline([

    ('scaler', StandardScaler()),

    ('classifier', SVC(kernel='linear'))

])
```

```
# Train and evaluate

pipeline.fit(X_train, y_train)

print("Accuracy:",      pipeline.score(X_test,
y_test))
```

Best Practice: Emphasize modularity and reusability in your pipeline design.

Scenario 4: Explaining Model Interpretability

Challenge: Explain why your model made a specific prediction.

Objective: Test your ability to communicate insights into model behavior.

Example Task: Use SHAP values to interpret predictions.

Solution:

python

```
import shap

from         sklearn.ensemble         import
RandomForestClassifier


# Train a model
```

```python
model = RandomForestClassifier()

model.fit(X_train, y_train)


# Explain predictions

explainer = shap.Explainer(model, X_train)

shap_values = explainer(X_test)


# Visualize SHAP values for a single prediction

shap.plots.waterfall(shap_values[0])
```

Best Practice: Link interpretability techniques to trustworthiness and business impact.

Key Takeaways

1. **Preparation:** Practice coding solutions and explaining decisions.
2. **Clarity:** Always connect technical solutions to real-world outcomes.
3. **Adaptability:** Tailor solutions to the specific scenario during interviews.

By mastering these common scenarios, you'll approach AI interviews with confidence and professionalism.

8.2 Sample Questions with Detailed Explanations

Preparing for an AI interview requires not only understanding the concepts but also practicing with diverse questions. This chapter provides carefully selected sample questions across critical AI domains. Each question is accompanied by a detailed explanation, demonstrating the reasoning and methodology for arriving at the solution.

Question 1: Data Imbalance in Classification Tasks

Problem:
You are working on a binary classification problem where the positive class is 10% of the dataset, and the negative class is 90%. How would you address this imbalance?

Explanation:
Data imbalance can bias the model toward predicting the majority class. Effective solutions include:

1. **Resampling Techniques:**
   - **Oversampling:** Increase the number of samples in the minority class using techniques like SMOTE (Synthetic Minority Oversampling Technique).
   - **Undersampling:** Reduce samples from the majority class to balance the dataset.
2. **Adjusting Class Weights:** Assign higher weights to the minority class during model training to penalize misclassification more heavily.
3. **Algorithm-Specific Techniques:** Use algorithms like XGBoost or Random Forest, which have built-in mechanisms for handling imbalance.

Code Example (Using Class Weights):

python

```python
from sklearn.ensemble import
RandomForestClassifier

from sklearn.model_selection import
train_test_split

from sklearn.metrics import
classification_report


# Simulated imbalanced dataset

X = [[i] for i in range(100)]

y = [0] * 90 + [1] * 10


# Split data

X_train, X_test, y_train, y_test =
train_test_split(X, y, test_size=0.2,
random_state=42)


# Train model with class weights

model =
RandomForestClassifier(class_weight='balanced
', random_state=42)

model.fit(X_train, y_train)
```

```
# Evaluate

y_pred = model.predict(X_test)

print(classification_report(y_test, y_pred))
```

Question 2: Explain Overfitting and How to Prevent It

Problem:
What is overfitting, and how can you prevent it when training machine learning models?

Explanation:
Overfitting occurs when a model performs well on training data but poorly on unseen data. It memorizes the training set rather than generalizing patterns.

Prevention Methods:

- **Regularization:** Add penalties to the loss function (e.g., L1 or L2 regularization).
- **Cross-Validation:** Evaluate model performance on unseen data during training.
- **Pruning:** For tree-based models, limit depth or number of leaves.
- **Data Augmentation:** Expand the dataset by generating variations of existing data.
- **Dropout (for Neural Networks):** Randomly deactivate neurons during training.

Code Example (Regularization):

python

```python
from sklearn.linear_model import Ridge

from sklearn.model_selection import
train_test_split

from sklearn.metrics import mean_squared_error


# Simulated dataset

X = [[i] for i in range(1, 21)]

y = [2*i + 1 for i in range(1, 21)]


# Split data

X_train, X_test, y_train, y_test =
train_test_split(X, y, test_size=0.2,
random_state=42)


# Ridge regression with L2 regularization

model = Ridge(alpha=1.0)

model.fit(X_train, y_train)


# Evaluate
```

```python
y_pred = model.predict(X_test)

print("MSE:",        mean_squared_error(y_test,
y_pred))
```

Question 3: Explain Backpropagation in Neural Networks

Problem:
Describe the backpropagation algorithm used for training neural networks.

Explanation:
Backpropagation updates weights in a neural network by minimizing the error between predicted and actual outputs.

1. **Forward Pass:** Compute output predictions.
2. **Loss Calculation:** Measure the difference between predictions and actual values using a loss function.
3. **Backward Pass:** Compute gradients of the loss with respect to each weight using the chain rule.
4. **Weight Update:** Adjust weights using gradient descent or its variants (e.g., Adam, RMSprop).

Code Example (Backpropagation Concept):

python

```python
import numpy as np

# Sigmoid function and its derivative

def sigmoid(x):

    return 1 / (1 + np.exp(-x))
```

```python
def sigmoid_derivative(x):
    return x * (1 - x)
# Input data
X = np.array([[0, 0], [0, 1], [1, 0], [1, 1]])
y = np.array([[0], [1], [1], [0]])


# Initialize weights
np.random.seed(42)
weights = np.random.rand(2, 1)
bias = np.random.rand(1)


# Training
learning_rate = 0.1
for epoch in range(10000):
    # Forward pass
    layer_1 = sigmoid(np.dot(X, weights) + bias)

    error = y - layer_1
```

```python
# Backpropagation

adjustments        =        error        *
sigmoid_derivative(layer_1)

weights  +=  np.dot(X.T,  adjustments)  *
learning_rate

bias      +=      np.sum(adjustments)      *
learning_rate


# Results

print("Trained Weights:", weights)

print("Trained Bias:", bias)
```

Question 4: What is Transfer Learning? Provide an Example.

Problem:
Explain transfer learning and its use cases.

Explanation:
Transfer learning involves using a pre-trained model as a starting point for a related task, reducing the need for large datasets and computational resources.

Example Use Case: Fine-tune a pre-trained ResNet model for classifying medical images.

Code Example:

python

```python
from tensorflow.keras.applications import ResNet50

from tensorflow.keras.models import Sequential

from tensorflow.keras.layers import Dense, Flatten

from tensorflow.keras.preprocessing.image import ImageDataGenerator


# Load pre-trained ResNet50 model

base_model = ResNet50(weights='imagenet', include_top=False, input_shape=(224, 224, 3))


# Build transfer learning model

model = Sequential([

    base_model,

    Flatten(),

    Dense(256, activation='relu'),

    Dense(1, activation='sigmoid')

])
```

```
# Freeze base model layers

base_model.trainable = False


# Compile and train

model.compile(optimizer='adam',
loss='binary_crossentropy',
metrics=['accuracy'])
```

Key Takeaways

- **Understand Core Concepts:** Each sample question highlights essential topics like data preprocessing, model training, and algorithm implementation.
- **Practice Code Writing:** Develop the ability to implement solutions efficiently.
- **Explain Decisions Clearly:** Communicate your reasoning during interviews to demonstrate competence.

This section equips you with practical tools and insights to tackle various challenges confidently during AI interviews.

8.3 Case Study: End-to-End Mock Interview with Model Deployment

This section walks through an end-to-end mock interview scenario involving designing, training, and deploying a machine learning model. The case study simulates a real-world problem, covering each step from understanding the problem requirements to deploying the solution.

Scenario: Predicting Customer Churn for a Subscription Service

You are asked to design a system that predicts customer churn for a subscription-based company. Your solution should demonstrate a clear understanding of the problem, data preprocessing, model development, evaluation, and deployment.

Step 1: Understanding the Problem

Problem **Statement:**
The task is to predict whether a customer will churn (i.e., cancel their subscription) based on historical customer data.

Key Deliverables:

1. A trained machine learning model capable of predicting churn.
2. A deployed REST API that serves the predictions.

Step 2: Data Preprocessing

Data **Overview:**
The dataset includes customer features like tenure, monthly charges, payment methods, and churn status.

Preprocessing Steps:

- Handle missing values.
- Encode categorical variables.

- Scale numerical features.

Code Example:

python

```
import pandas as pd

from       sklearn.model_selection       import
train_test_split

from       sklearn.preprocessing       import
StandardScaler, LabelEncoder


# Load dataset

data = pd.read_csv("customer_churn.csv")


# Handle missing values

data.fillna(data.mean(), inplace=True)


# Encode categorical variables

encoder = LabelEncoder()

data['PaymentMethod']                             =
encoder.fit_transform(data['PaymentMethod'])


# Scale numerical features
```

```
scaler = StandardScaler()

data[['Tenure',     'MonthlyCharges']]      =
scaler.fit_transform(data[['Tenure',
'MonthlyCharges']])



# Split dataset

X = data.drop('Churn', axis=1)

y = data['Churn']

X_train,    X_test,    y_train,    y_test    =
train_test_split(X,      y,      test_size=0.2,
random_state=42)
```

Step 3: Model Development

Model   Selection:
For this task, we use a Random Forest classifier due to its
robustness and interpretability.

Training the Model:

python

```
from sklearn.ensemble import
RandomForestClassifier

from sklearn.metrics import
classification_report
```

```python
# Train model

model                                      =
RandomForestClassifier(random_state=42)

model.fit(X_train, y_train)


# Evaluate model

y_pred = model.predict(X_test)

print(classification_report(y_test, y_pred))
```

Step 4: Model Optimization

To improve performance, use hyperparameter tuning with GridSearchCV.

Code Example:

python

```python
from sklearn.model_selection import
GridSearchCV


# Hyperparameter grid

param_grid = {
```

```
    'n_estimators': [100, 200],

    'max_depth': [10, 20],

    'min_samples_split': [2, 5]

}


# GridSearch

grid_search                                    =
GridSearchCV(RandomForestClassifier(random_st
ate=42), param_grid, cv=3)

grid_search.fit(X_train, y_train)


# Best model

best_model = grid_search.best_estimator_

print("Best                        Parameters:",
grid_search.best_params_)
```

Step 5: Deployment

Deploy the model using Flask to create a REST API that serves predictions.

Code for Deployment:

python

```python
from flask import Flask, request, jsonify
import pickle

# Save model
with open("model.pkl", "wb") as f:
    pickle.dump(best_model, f)

# Load model
with open("model.pkl", "rb") as f:
    loaded_model = pickle.load(f)

# Flask app
app = Flask(__name__)

@app.route('/predict', methods=['POST'])
def predict():
    data = request.get_json()
```

```python
    features = [data['Tenure'],
data['MonthlyCharges'],
data['PaymentMethod']]

    prediction =
loaded_model.predict([features])

    return jsonify({'Churn':
int(prediction[0])})


if __name__ == '__main__':

    app.run(debug=True)
```

Step 6: Testing the Deployment

Use `curl` or tools like Postman to test the API:

bash

```bash
curl -X POST -H "Content-Type:
application/json" -d '{"Tenure": 12,
"MonthlyCharges": 50, "PaymentMethod": 1}'
http://127.0.0.1:5000/predict
```

Expected Output:

json

```json
{

  "Churn": 0

}
```

Interview Discussion Points

1. **Explain Model Choice:** Justify why you chose Random Forest for this problem.
2. **Tradeoffs:** Discuss challenges in hyperparameter tuning and deployment.
3. **Scalability:** Address how the solution scales for real-time predictions.
4. **Evaluation Metrics:** Highlight the importance of precision, recall, and F1-score.

Key Takeaways

- **Showcase Breadth:** An end-to-end solution demonstrates your versatility in handling data, algorithms, and deployment.
- **Communicate Clearly:** Present each step logically during the interview.
- **Prepare for Questions:** Be ready to explain decisions, optimizations, and possible improvements.

By practicing this comprehensive case study, you can build the confidence to navigate complex interview scenarios effectively.

Chapter 9: Negotiation and Career Growth in AI

This chapter focuses on strategies for navigating job offers, long-term career planning, and lessons from successful AI professionals. Whether you're negotiating your first offer or building a sustainable career, this chapter provides actionable insights tailored to AI professionals.

9.1 Tips for Negotiating Job Offers

Assessing the Offer

Understand the full scope of a job offer beyond salary, including benefits, equity, bonuses, learning opportunities, and work-life balance. Evaluate:

- Base salary: Industry benchmarks using platforms like Glassdoor or Levels.fyi.
- Benefits: Health insurance, paid leave, and relocation packages.
- Growth opportunities: Availability of mentorship, resources for skill-building, and room for promotions.

Checklist for Assessment:

1. Compensation vs. market standards.
2. Career growth potential.
3. Alignment with long-term goals.

Strategies for Negotiation

Prepare Your Value Proposition:
Highlight your skills, achievements, and how you can

contribute to the company. Use metrics where possible, e.g., "improved model accuracy by 15%."

Negotiation Techniques:

- Use anchoring: Set a reasonable but higher-than-expected number based on research.
- Be collaborative: Frame negotiations as seeking mutual benefit.
- Have a BATNA (Best Alternative to a Negotiated Agreement): Know your fallback options.

Example Dialogue for Negotiation:
Hiring Manager: "The offer is $120,000."
You: "I appreciate the offer. Based on industry standards and my experience in optimizing AI models that increased efficiency by 20%, I was expecting something closer to $140,000. Could we align closer to that range?"

Avoiding Common Pitfalls

- **Don't Rush:** Ask for time to evaluate the offer.
- **Don't Focus Solely on Salary:** Highlight other aspects like projects and learning opportunities.
- **Don't Forget Culture Fit:** Ensure alignment with the company's mission and values.

9.2 Building a Long-Term Career Path in AI

Developing Core Competencies

AI careers require constant skill upgrades. Prioritize:

- Technical Depth: Master key topics like neural networks, NLP, and reinforcement learning.

- Domain Knowledge: Gain expertise in industries like healthcare, finance, or robotics.
- Communication: Learn to explain complex AI concepts to non-technical stakeholders.

Exploring Career Paths

AI professionals have diverse career paths, including:

- **Research Scientist:** Focus on publishing and pushing the boundaries of AI.
- **Machine Learning Engineer:** Develop deployable AI systems.
- **Product Manager (AI):** Manage AI solutions for business needs.
- **AI Consultant:** Offer specialized knowledge across projects.

Case Study:
Jane transitioned from a data scientist to an AI product manager by developing her leadership skills and learning the business impact of AI.

Embracing Lifelong Learning

- Follow emerging trends (e.g., generative AI, federated learning).
- Engage in open-source projects or competitions (e.g., Kaggle).
- Join AI communities for networking and mentoring.

9.3 Real-Life Examples from Successful AI Professionals

Example 1: Transition to AI Leadership

John started as a machine learning engineer and transitioned to VP of AI Strategy. His steps included:

1. Developing team leadership skills.
2. Driving strategic AI projects that resulted in cost savings.
3. Building cross-functional collaborations.

Example 2: Overcoming Early Challenges

Amara faced challenges breaking into AI due to limited experience. She:

1. Built a strong portfolio through personal projects, like an NLP chatbot.
2. Networked at AI conferences, landing an internship.
3. Used her first role to specialize in NLP, eventually joining a top AI lab.

Lessons Learned:

- Leverage opportunities to demonstrate your impact.
- Seek mentorship to navigate challenges and seize opportunities.

Final Thoughts

Navigating a successful AI career requires strategic planning, strong technical skills, and effective communication. Whether negotiating an offer or envisioning long-term growth, approach each decision with research and confidence. Learning from real-world examples can inspire actionable steps toward sustained success in AI.

Conclusion

This final chapter consolidates the insights gained throughout the book and provides actionable advice for adapting to the ever-evolving field of artificial intelligence. It equips readers with the tools to continuously learn, prepare for emerging trends, and achieve long-term success in their AI careers.

Recap of Key Insights

Over the course of this book, we have explored:

- **Foundational Knowledge:** Understanding core AI concepts, algorithms, and models.
- **Hands-On Skills:** Developing practical expertise through coding, model optimization, and deployment.
- **Problem-Solving Techniques:** Approaches to tackle algorithmic and real-world AI challenges.
- **Interview Strategies:** Excelling in technical and behavioral AI interviews with confidence.
- **Career Development:** Crafting a sustainable career path through negotiation, skill growth, and networking.

Each chapter has emphasized practical examples, real-world applications, and actionable strategies to ensure readiness for AI interviews and beyond.

Preparing for Future Trends in AI

Adapting to Technological Shifts

AI is a dynamic field with rapid advancements. Staying current with trends like:

- **Generative AI:** Advances in transformer models (e.g., GPT, BERT) for creative tasks.
- **Ethical AI:** Addressing bias, privacy, and fairness in AI applications.
- **Edge Computing:** Deploying AI models on devices for low-latency solutions.

Action Steps:

1. Regularly review research papers on platforms like arXiv.
2. Follow thought leaders and industry blogs.
3. Engage in online courses and certifications for cutting-edge skills.

Building an Adaptive Mindset

The AI landscape demands continuous learning and flexibility:

- **Experimentation:** Participate in hackathons or build passion projects.
- **Interdisciplinary Learning:** Integrate AI with fields like robotics, healthcare, or climate science.
- **Networking:** Join AI conferences, webinars, and professional communities.

Leveraging AI for Career Growth

Use AI tools to advance your professional journey:

- Develop personal branding with AI-powered analytics on platforms like LinkedIn.
- Automate repetitive tasks in your workflow, enhancing productivity.

- Create an online portfolio showcasing your AI projects and achievements.

Success in AI requires a blend of technical expertise, adaptability, and strategic career planning. This book has equipped you with the knowledge and tools to crack AI interviews and thrive in this competitive industry. Your journey in AI doesn't end here; it's a lifelong process of growth, innovation, and impact.

Stay curious, stay committed, and continue pushing the boundaries of what AI can achieve. The future of AI is in your hands.

Appendix

Glossary of AI Terms

This section provides concise definitions of essential AI-related terminology to ensure readers have a clear understanding of key concepts:

- **Artificial Intelligence (AI):** Simulation of human intelligence in machines programmed to think, reason, and learn.
- **Neural Network:** A computational model inspired by the structure of the human brain, used in deep learning.
- **Supervised Learning:** A type of machine learning where models are trained on labeled data.
- **Hyperparameter Tuning:** Adjusting model settings to optimize performance.
- **Overfitting:** A model's performance degrades by learning noise rather than underlying patterns.

Courses:

- Coursera's Machine Learning by Andrew Ng
- Stanford's CS231n: Convolutional Neural Networks for Visual Recognition
- fast.ai's Practical Deep Learning for Coders

Tools and Frameworks:

- **TensorFlow** and **PyTorch:** Leading frameworks for AI and machine learning.
- **Jupyter Notebooks:** Ideal for exploratory programming.
- **Kaggle:** A platform for datasets, competitions, and collaborative learning.

www.ingramcontent.com/pod-product-compliance
Lightning Source LLC
LaVergne TN
LVHW080116070326
832902LV00015B/2616